Plato's Peach

Previous books by John Freeman

Poetry

Snow Corridors, Rivelin Press, Sheffield, 1975

A Landscape Out of Focus, Galloping Dog Press, Swansea, 1978

The Unseizable, Stone Lantern Press, Swansea, 1978

A Vase of Honesty, Great Works Editions, Bishop's Stortford, 1979

Going Home, Rivelin Press, Bradford, 1984

The Light is of Love, I Think: New and Selected Poems, Stride Publications, Exeter, 1997

Landscape With Portraits, Redbeck Press, Bradford, 1999

A Suite For Summer, Worple Press, Tonbridge, 2007

White Wings: New and Selected Prose Poems, Contraband Books, London, 2013

Strata Smith and the Anthropocene, The Knives Forks and Spoons Press, Newton-le-Willows, 2016

What Possessed Me, Worple Press, Tonbridge, 2016

Criticism

The Less Received: Neglected Modern Poets, Stride Publications, Exeter, 2000

PLATO'S PEACH

JOHN FREEMAN

First published in 2021 by
Worple Press
www.worplepress.co.uk

Printed by imprintdigital
Upton Pyne, Exeter
www.digital.imprint.co.uk

Typesetting and cover design by The Book Typesetters
us@thebooktypesetters.com
07422 598 168
www.thebooktypesetters.com

ISBN 978-1-905208-46-3

Acknowledgements

Some of these poems or earlier versions of them have appeared or will appear in the following magazines, and I am grateful to the editors and publishers concerned: *Agenda*, *Confluence*, *Littoral*, *London Grip*, *Poetry Wales*, *Raceme*, *Scintilla*, *Sentinel Literary Quarterly*, *Stand*, *Tears in the Fence*, *The Frogmore Papers*, *The Journal*, *The Lonely Crowd*.

Some of the other poems or earlier versions of them have appeared in the following anthologies, and I am again grateful to the editors and publishers: *At Time's Edge: Remembering Anne Cluysenaar* (The Vaughan Association, 2016), *Poems for Jeremy Corbyn* (Shoestring Press, 2016), *The Bridport Prize Anthology, 2018* and *2020* (Redcliff Press), *The Tree Line: Poems for Trees, Woods, & People* (Worple Press, 2017), *Ware Poets 20th Competition Anthology, 2018*.

'Exhibition' won the Bridport Poetry Prize, 2018, and 'Vee Oit' was highly commended in the Bridport Prize competition, 2020. 'Opus 131' won second prize in the Sentinel Literary Quarterly Poetry Competition, February 2018.

I am grateful for supportive and constructive criticism on drafts of these poems from Ruth Calway, Jonathan Edwards, Henry Lyman, Michael McKimm, Janet Peters, Linda Saunders, and especially from Vivien Freeman, who is present in many of these poems, and without whom they would not have been possible.

The lyrics of 'Du Gris,' quoted in '*Eh Monsieur, une Cigarette…*' on page 60 are by Ernest Dumont. The music was written by Ferdinand-Louis Bénech and the song was made famous by Berthe Sylva. There are YouTube recordings of Sylva and several later interpreters performing it, including Marlene Dietrich and Renaud. The lines quoted from Rainer Maria Rilke in 'Being There' on page 141 are from the first of his *Duino Elegies*. The passage quoted from a letter by Rilke in 'Two Women' on page 176 is taken from the notes to the edition of Rilke's *Sonnets to Orpheus* translated by M.D. Herter Norton and published by

W.W. Norton (p.138). The poem by Anne Cluysenaar quoted in 'Time Perpetually Revolving' (page 165) is 'Near the Farmers Arms, Llandegfedd' from her collection *Migrations* (Cinnamon Press, 2011, p.38).

Contents

3: Country Dancing

4: A Sky Reflected

5: Visiting Giverny

6: Time Perpetually Revolving

1: My Life In Trees

The Beautiful River

I never saw him dance exactly, not,
that is, waltz or do the foxtrot, let alone
the jive of a later generation, nor
the shuffle from foot to foot under dim light
of what I learned to call in French *un slow*.
And yet it's almost as a dancer now
he comes back to me, or at any rate
I sense his presence as he was, compact,
gracefully inhabiting his body,
warm and, though slight, utterly substantial,
a body permeated and in harmony
with a spirit watchful and humane.
He wore the wisdom of experience –
two world wars, the Great Depression, illness,
and his wage slavery, as he called it once,
though teaching never ceased to be for him
a passion, a vocation, and a gift –
wearing all this and more, lightly, as lightly
as his Terylene trousers with their turn-ups,
nylon shirts and knitted cardigans.

He never lost affection for the hymns
he learned in childhood, though he called himself
atheist, rationalist, and humanist.
Yes, I'll sing of my redeemer, he would say
suddenly in the midst of a long silence,
earnestly, pottering round the house,
or, forbid it Lord, that I should boast.
He put real feeling into the word con-*tempt*
when he said he poured it on all his pride.
But there was always that poised doubleness,
the sending up as well as paying homage,
as when he said, to the work, to the work,
we are servants of Gawd, or sang, quite nicely,
shall we gather at the river, and bent
his knees and flicked a slim hip sideways

in an understated sexy wiggle
each time he came to the first syllable
of the repeated word in the refrain,
the *beau*-tiful, the *beau*-tiful *ri*–i–ver.

Net Curtains

The white net curtains in the dining room
were nylon, light in the breeze, harsh to the touch,
a mesh bunched evenly along the wire
that stretched across each of the lower sashes
from hook to hook screwed into the woodwork
by the presiding spirit of the house.
She had painted the panelling a warm
light yellow gloss to match the slightly paler
emulsion on the papered walls and darker
Anaglypta below the waist-high rail. She
made the bookcases, the meals, the running when
visitors stimulated conversation
around the table where we paid her homage.

There were times when no one else was present
and I sat in that room alone, feeling
the silence all around me, watching the light
fall on and partly through the clean net curtains,
with dust motes in a beam the sun was casting
through the clear panes in the upper sashes,
or one of them, below the frosted panels.
The motes seemed to be rising more than falling,
lovely in the eye of the beholder
reflecting on a parable not quite
understood from that morning's Bible reading,
at lunch time in this interval before
I trotted back alone along the road
for the afternoon of busy lessons.
But they took on a melancholy meaning
from the stasis, with the sun bringing to light
the slow dance of the only things that moved
in the house at that moment, and from the sound
of children in a school nearer than mine
at play, their sharp cries in the middle distance
softened and blended into a single

low roar, but with high points of excitement,
the world as joyful social gathering.

Years passed, and I found my socialising
and loneliness in other private spaces
and public ones, but I went back when I could,
till the genius of the place collapsed
one October evening in the kitchen.

I know what had made up the solitude
of which she had too much in her last decade.
I think of it, and her, and see the dust motes,
hear the children playing in their lunch hour,
and visualise with a sharp clarity
steel circles at the end of the stout wires
tense with the strain of holding up those curtains.

A Square of Chocolate

For Michael Freeman

What I've got to say means I must tell you
about a square of Cadbury's milk chocolate, dropped
by my big brother and our hero, Michael,
between his bed and mine early one morning,
when he was pushing thirteen. I was five.
Or I was six and he was nearly fourteen.
Whichever. Makes no difference to the story.
I'm here to tell this lovely company,
gathered to celebrate his special birthday,
now that we're both older, just a little,
something you don't already know about him.
Some of you first encountered Michael, Mike,
as a fellow cricketer, fellow student,
as actor, manager, or actor-manager,
father, grandfather, in-law, friend, or uncle,
but none of you will have had the same parents,
and lived in the same house when you were children.

So. It all centres on this piece of chocolate.
I've just woken up and I'm still sleepy.
For years I've had my eyes on Michael's trainset,
a clockwork Hornby thing with chunky rails,
goods wagons and a heavy locomotive
I've sometimes been allowed to help him play with
across the lino, or the grass in summer,
and being only little, a bit clumsy,
I've sometimes trodden on the rails and bent them,
which, in a way a whole later succession
of children will be familiar with, some
of them now big strapping lads, some parents,
Michael responded to with a judicious
balance of severity and kindness,
so that I was filled with melancholy,
and a determination to do better.

As well as trains, Michael had Dinky Toys,
model motor cars, taxis and lorries,
enough to fill a city centre with,
or so it seemed to my imagination
when there were fewer real cars on the streets,
and I was little, and not good at counting.
I had a few of these Dinkies myself,
all of them duplicates of his, but we knew
which were which, because his were perfect,
and mine had missing tyres, or wonky wheels,
bits chipped off the paint or a lamp broken.
It was my birthday, and my elder brother
though not, except in my admiring eyes,
arrived at manhood, had decided this
was the time to put away his childish things,
and that maybe I was almost old enough
to be trusted not to wreck all of them,
though he hadn't given me a hint of this,
any more than he'd answered my entreaties
to say what he was making, when I saw him
whittling away at bits of balsa wood
under the apple tree in the back garden,
and just grinning when I said, oh *tell* me,
jumping up and down in my frustration.

So there I am in the morning, waking up,
and there is Michael saying, happy birthday,
passing me a square from an eight-ounce slab
of chocolate which I reach to take from him
when he, who's taught me how to catch a ball
and calls me butterfingers if I drop one,
accidentally drops the square of chocolate
so that I look down and see a railway
stretching under his bed one way, under mine
the other, and in the middle the most
ingenious level crossing he has made
out of two lengths of track, and wood, and cardboard,
painted brown, and white, and red, with verges
of green on the sloping bits of roadway,

with all his cars lined up on the two sides
of the gates along the corridor between us,
and somehow makes me know that this is mine.

Sometimes brothers fall out, annoy each other,
and I don't say we've never had such moments,
but when Carl asked if I would say something,
and preferably make a poem of it,
to help celebrate his hero and mine,
I knew I had to speak about the moment
I was filled with love and adoration
by what I saw when Michael accidentally
on purpose dropped a little square of chocolate.

Walking Under Trees

There were plane trees growing from the pavement
at intervals along my road to school,
with slabs of stone omitted to make space
so that their trunks had room to breathe and burgeon.
The boles were dappled, once with sunlight filtered
through broad and well-spaced leaves like open hands,
and twice with bark patterned in two colours.
They rose like fountains to cascade in branches,
and dandle in the breeze their waving fans
with pendants like soft versions of spiked maces.

Turning from our front door the other way
on Sundays, we crossed one road, then another,
and found ourselves beyond some high black railings
where paths led us quickly to a circle
of the tallest and most self-expressive
plane trees I'd seen, or can remember seeing,
their unpruned branches reaching out and stretching
in all directions, making a *temenos*,
though I'd never met the word, nor even
in English heard the phrase *a sacred grove*.

I was a constant fidget during lessons,
so when at my new school we learned about
teachers and students walking under trees,
Plato's Academy, I felt quite certain
that was the way to do it, to keep moving,
drinking in wisdom from the trees and elders.
How would I have felt if they had told me
that among the olives there were plane trees?

Best not to have had that knowledge interfere,
or seem to shape the feeling I developed
for that circle where I walked so often
with someone who addressed me as an equal,
and formed my mental landscape, and with whom

I picked up fallen leaves to see the difference
between them and the leaves of sycamores,
or in the same park, as we walked on, talking,
the birch, the beech, the lime, the graceful ash.

Sharing Sweets on a Station Platform

When I see loose-limbed, graceful cricketers
from Trinidad, Jamaica or Barbados,
I think of men I used to meet in childhood,
bus drivers and conductors, railway porters,
or crowding Brixton market where I went
to buy potatoes, apples, greens and grapefruit
from a list given me by my mother.
It was the friendliest, safest place I knew.
What shocked me when I opened an account
at a bank was hearing tellers making jokes,
not caring if I heard them, that weren't funny
but full of ugly spite about their neighbours.
I saw nothing to like in either of them.
I wouldn't call their unwholesome colour white,
just unhealthy, pallid like curdled milk
or something else that ought to be thrown out.
I thought back to when I'd been much younger,
standing on platform 2 at Herne Hill, taking
a fruit gum from a packet, peeling it back
to offer to somebody who was with me.
A railway worker built like Joel Garner
happened to be walking along the track.
I caught his eye and offered him a fruit gum.
Tall as he was, his face was just below me.
I peeled the paper back. His hands were dirty,
he showed me, so I put into his mouth
the small round ridged jelly like a wafer,
as he looked up with a face as trusting
as I was myself or even more so.
Don't think I'm saying that he wasn't adult.
I'm sure people like those clerks had got to him.
He was touched, I saw, and made me feel I'd done
something beautiful, but to me it was he
who was beautiful, a spirit full of grace.

I hope that moment shone through years of insult for him as it has always done for me.

Plato's Peach

I wonder whether Plato got his notion
of ideal archetypes of everything
from early memories of first encounters,
such as the time a woman dressed in black
offered him a peach out of her basket
when they were riding in the same conveyance,
and he shyly refused out of politeness
but she insisted, don't you like peaches?
He couldn't deny he did, and she held out
the most enormous, dark, perfectly ripe
and yet not over-ripe example of
a peach he'd ever seen, and so he took it,
and felt the weight of it, and saw the bloom
on its dusky red and purple, almost black,
silky covering and began to eat it,
finding it of a consistent texture,
yielding but firm, not mushy nor gone over,
full of juice which somehow stayed united
with the yellow flesh and didn't dribble.
Did every nerve and taste-bud on his young
unjaded palate reach a pitch of pleasure
as astonished as it was delighted,
so that he had a dawning intimation
of unsuspected different ways of being?
In later years did Plato try ripe peaches,
never recapturing, always reminded
of a journey otherwise forgotten
between his native Athens and say, Delphi,
and the quintessential peach of childhood
pressed on him by a woman in dark clothes,
until he knew that beyond our senses
there must be the one perfect exemplar
of everything that we discover round us,
tables, apples, horses, boats and fishes,
which these copies half make present to us?
For myself the thought of peaches leads me

back to the green leather-covered benches
of a train rocking southwards deep in France
throughout eternity, as it seems to me,
and a woman in mourning saying, take it.

Marching Orders

For Jonathan Edwards

I'm standing staring at the apple tree,
the fissured bark six inches from my eyes.
Behind it are the sitting room's French windows
and next to them, below my dark back bedroom,
the bricks whose pointing I have worn away
by tossing tennis balls at them to hit
with a cricket stump, keeping a straight bat.
It's as if the satisfying texture
of this familiar apple tree's rough skin
is speaking to me on behalf of something
that includes the solid, silent house, the sky
above it, and something intangible.

The house, the tree, the garden, everything
is an expression of my Mum and Dad.
There never were such peculiar people,
or so it seems to me. I have survived
discovering I'm living in a madhouse,
and being deeply embarrassed and ashamed
of how each of them has a unique talent
for being quite ridiculous in public.
I know this will continue, while they live,
whenever I am in their company
with anyone normal, but I also know
that there is something infinite about them.
Each of them is particular and varied
like a long novel or an epic poem,
a city you set out to feel you've mastered
and find you never can come to the end of.
I know nobody knows this except me.
Neither of them will ever become famous,
which shows how empty being famous is.

The tree, this bit of the brown bark, just here
where the lines flow around a small grey knot,
is telling me something. It surprises me.

I have been put on earth to write about them,
to preserve, not just their memory, but them.
Under the dull routines of daily living
I have seen, and once I've seen it can't un-see,
the welling up of an unending richness.
This secret source makes all the details precious;
the source wouldn't be real without the details.

It occurs to me, while this is happening,
that I might have had other intentions.
There's so much to discover in the world
apart from this, which I've known all my life.
So I'm not overjoyed, and not excited.
Neither do I panic or feel trapped. The tree
is speaking in me very quietly.
The moment comes and goes without high drama.

It's so discreet I might not even guess
that I will go on remembering this
unexpected, unsought visitation
till I'm much older than my parents are,
so long, in fact, that it is safe to say
that while I can remember anything
I'll recall getting my surprising orders,
and how from time to time I've followed them.

Plato says that we begin by loving
an individual, then a class of beings,
then institutions, finally ideas,
in a sense beyond our usual meaning.
What I saw in those two people helps me see
in everyone I meet, or get to know,
not as much detail, but the same essentials,
unfathomable, beyond price or judgement.
Sometimes they too seem to demand my witness.

Swapping the Spools

It was always a surprise. The key you struck,
its capital in white on a black disk
under your finger, F or W,
would only yield so far and then resist,
and the metallic arm, a prodded snake
rising from a nest of sleeping serpents,
would freeze at its zenith like the picture
of the accomplice of a turbaned charmer,
its heavy head unable to reach forward
and sting or kiss the sheet of foolscap paper
through the long black veil of the inked ribbon.
The spools themselves, which until then had turned
like the rotating cogs of the insides
of an old-fashioned clock in a stone tower,
were jammed, the central cylinder of one
naked but for the final nylon circlet,
sewn to itself to stop it slipping off.
However absorbed you might be, composing
a letter, say, or copying a poem,
the unresponsive key, the thwarted cobra,
the uncompleted word above the tape,
all told you plainly that you had to stop
and lift the shiny metal holders out,
turn them over, fiddle to re-insert
the slackened silkiness between the struts
which hoisted it to where the steel would strike
and press shaped blackness up against the page,
held in place by a stationary roller.
Manage it if you can, it's quite a challenge,
without inking your fingers and transferring
smudged patterns to the glossy keys or paper.
Now carry on with what you had been doing,
the sound of thunder telling the whole house
you're at the front room dining table, clacking
on the big, second-hand Imperial,
with the v that always sticks and must be

prised off the page, and an e which doesn't print, that inconv ni ntly common l tter.

A Hand of Crib

Did you shuffle these cards wasn't a question,
it was a rhetoric of disappointment.
Take these cards back, he'd say, scanning the hand
I'd dealt him in the overheated room
where I went fortnightly to visit him,
or, Mother, was it worth it. After each round
he'd count, and soon I learned how to say it:
fifteen two, fifteen four, and a pair is six,
and, if he had a Jack, one for his nob.
I'll take a large amount of nineteen meant
no points, and if I'd gone first with a score
better than his he said, with the same deadpan
expression he kept to almost always,
after the Lord Mayor's show comes the dung cart.
I must, he said, smartly lifting himself
sideways out of his winged armchair to let out
a little fart I might have scarcely heard
if he hadn't alerted me beforehand.
I came to anticipate the moment
when he'd progress slowly past me to the hall,
open the wardrobe where he kept the hat
and coat he hardly ever wore in those days,
pull out the bottle of White Horse, bring it in,
and though his hand shook fill two little glasses
up to the brim and never spill a drop.
He raised his toward the ceiling, said gravely,
success to temperance, and tipped it down.
Your aunt will be in directly, he said,
glancing at the clock. Nobody else said that.
I'd grown up with the idioms and accents
of south London and the East End in my ears,
but come across 'directly' only in books.
I hadn't realised that vernaculars,
like more formal registers, change over time.
I thought Sam Weller's funny way of saying
w for v must have been made up,

until I heard this man born in the year
Charles Dickens died say, laying his cards down,
as he must have said all his life, wery good.

Properly Drunk

What it can have been that made me say that
I don't know, but in lessons I hated
I used to look out dumbly through the window
of the airless second-storey classroom
at the row of lofty pine-trees swaying
in the wind, and want to be among them,
and on solitary evenings I would walk
under the limes along the road that winds
past a small wood and college playing fields,
reciting to myself with gusty passion.
The winter branches of a full-grown beech
were silhouetted by a lamplight's silver
as if by moonlight, which I thought it was
the first time I saw it, against whiteness,
the high blank end-wall of the alms houses.

Whatever the reason was, when I left school
at last and landed in another city,
a part of it with not a blade of grass
nor a sparrow, nor anything else living
that wasn't either verminous or human,
or both together, my almost only
happy memory or, if that's too sweeping,
the only one which I could call euphoric,
was when I found myself at someone's party
in a house on a leafy avenue,
and a kind girl, much savvier than I was,
plumpish and blonde, cuddled me and snogged me
with warm wet kisses I can still remember,
probably not intending anything
at all more than that and, novice that I was,
I'd have been terrified if I'd thought she did,
even if I hadn't been, for the first time
in my life, properly drunk, as well as,
for the first time also, locked in an embrace,
rolling gently on the carpet, saying

22

repeatedly, when my mouth was disengaged,
sometimes breaking off indeed from kissing
to say, and say again, whatever it was
I meant by it, I want to be a tree.

Light in Darkness

The record player from home had a small light,
a pea-sized yellow bulb which shone quite dimly
through the mesh of synthetic fabric
covering the speaker at one end. I'd bought
cheap, not knowing anything about it,
except that the music was by Beethoven,
an L. P. with a picture on the sleeve
of a spectacular midwinter sunset
over the silhouetted scaffolding
of a dock, some sort of pier. Sky and sea
were sombre, and as if suffused with blood.
Chiming with the image on the cover
was how I felt about walking the streets
of that city, spoken to by no-one
except an old woman asking for money,
cold greyness and November twilight round us.
And then one Sunday I took myself off
to a melancholy country landscape
and mooched around it for an afternoon.
all this blended with that random record,
the picture, the austere, unearthly music.
I recalled something Goethe had written:
art is like stained glass, to see its colours
you need to look at it from inside darkness.
I sat on the edge of my bed and waited,
mesmerised by that cover photograph,
as the needle gently settled in the groove
and the first notes of the slow, rising tune
on the first violin, reflective, seeking
yet also offering redress, began
what I would never listen to again
without a sense of treading holy ground,
and a memory, sometimes more conscious,
sometimes less, of the little yellow light
shining from the ancient record player
on the round table in the tall bay window,

and fading daylight from the treeless street
falling on that picture of a sunset.

Stealing Away

I wonder if they thought I'd picked their pockets,
the two women whose cases I had carried
after noticing that they were struggling
and having time to spare before my train left.
We chatted as we walked. I don't remember
what we said, only that it was human.
I was eighteen, living away from home
for the first time, and on an empty Sunday
had taken myself out of one city
to walk around another's walls and markets
and its cathedral, and some lonely fields
where twilight overtook me among reed beds.
I blew on embers of the consolations
I found here and there, a tutting blackbird,
a treasured ring in a museum case,
and now this simple civilised exchange.
I went with them into their booked compartment
on an express, happy to be of service,
and watched them as they turned their backs towards me,
bending over handbags, looking, I could tell,
for a tip they thought I must have wanted.
Each time since then when I've been disappointed
in some hope of friendly understanding
I've seen those two old ladies rummaging
rather slowly in their calculations.
Silently I left, hoping that when they turned
they would come to know their helper better.
I felt sorry for them, but knew the loser
was me, the one to whom it mattered. Still,
as well as sadness and the cold return
of the November mist of isolation,
there was the sense that what I'd done had been
its own reward, making my prison larger.
What did the ladies think, when they looked round,
having worked out how much they ought to offer?
Did they suspect they'd undervalued me?

Or did they check to see, thinking my fingers
might have moved as quickly and as lightly
as my departing footsteps, nothing was missing?

Lighting Up England

During the England scene they needed me
there in the light box, perhaps the highest space
where anybody worked in the whole building.
Usually the man in charge could cope,
but so many spots and floods had to come up
at once when the scene began and then down
at the end it took two pairs of hands in sync.
I liked the unassuming electrician.
He had the self-respect and confidence
of somebody who knows what he's about
and doesn't restlessly want to be elsewhere.

The director had decided the whole show
except for this one scene ought to be creepy,
take place in varying degrees of darkness.
Perhaps that was why, someone suggested,
the Scottish play had always been unlucky –
when nobody can see what they are doing
they're bound to make mistakes, fall over things.
The England scene was lit with all we'd got.
It seemed almost a play within a play.

I was glad to be able to relax,
peer through the window, look down to the stage,
the tiny actors standing there in costume,
the Tannoy bringing speeches to my ear
and to the substrate of my consciousness,
to come out in after years as maxims.
Contemplating certain of our leaders
I've recalled, *fit to govern? No, not to live.*
Answering messages from friends I've written
more than once, when summing up my feelings,
*such welcome and unwelcome things at once
'tis hard to reconcile.* It often is.

And yet for me the words bring back good moments –
a rare companionship, a relaxation,
having nothing to do for twenty minutes
but look and listen to immortal speeches,
knowing that I was, above the people
in the stalls and circle, up in the gods,
myself, for that short time, a being of light.

The Work Camp in Alsace

We boys and young men had an army tent
with a row of identical camp beds
down each side and a walkway in the middle.
It was a high enough space to stand up in.
There was a caravan where the girl apart
who ran the stores kept her unenvied state.
A small old-fashioned house had one big room
downstairs with long trestle tables in it
end to end where we sat to eat our meals.
Above it in a world I never entered
was the girls' dormitory. On the last night
there was going to be a fire and a dance.
Outside, we noticed the upstairs light was on,
something that never happened otherwise.
We saw shadows moving across the blind.
One of us said, *les jeunes filles se font belles*,
the girls are making themselves beautiful.
What they all looked like with their makeup on
I don't remember, not even one of them.
I preferred their faces as I knew them.
And yet there was enchantment in that moment,
the mystique of womanhood, the poignancy
of their deliberate attempts at glamour,
and of our propensity, if not then,
at other times before or after that one,
to fall for it and some time to fall hard,
all softened by the fact that nobody
was about to fall for anyone tonight.
Those who were going to pair off had done so.
We were all friends, most of us liked each other.
We boys were touched by the seriousness
with which the girls went through a ritual
we could think of with benign detachment,
reminded that, familiar as they seemed,
they were unfathomably different from us.

Degrees and Classes

They were discreet about it, the wealthier
among my student friends, knowing better
than to consume conspicuously. One
had brown paper parcels delivered in which
laundered and ironed shirts lay neatly folded.
He holidayed in Mexico that winter,
but kept it quiet when we reconvened,
drinking instant coffee after dinner
with the rest of us until we groaned, parted,
and went back to staring at our essays.
One New Yorker friend cut short another,
telling him with sardonic certainty,
compared to people you'll meet here, you're rich.
With girls, or women, whichever they were –
I was just a boy, and naïve with it –
books, naturally, since we were all readers,
came into it. I gave one a slim volume
as a birthday present or for Christmas which
she said she'd treasure as it came from me,
though her father had opened an account
at a shop, so she could have anything
she wanted for her studies or amusement.
She decided I was history before
inviting me to her parents' London home
for a party flowing with the best champagne
at the end of one term, but didn't tell me
till the start of next, though her friends all knew.
That woman from Wisconsin who took me
off the shelf, and studied me for six months,
before shutting me up and putting me down,
left me with the memory of reading
together from my second-hand editions
of *Little Dorrit* and *Bleak House* and *Dombey*,
and a late glimpse of her own larger-print,
glossy-jacketed, New Oxford hardback,
with silver tooling and the illustrations

by Phiz, with which I saw her disappear
into an elegant Georgian residence
for visiting graduates, and close the door.

Dicing with Death

Not so fast, not so fast, he said, the first words
I'd heard from him since he'd been lying there,
so I thought it might be a revival,
a coming back to consciousness and health.
As he spoke his fingers moved quite nimbly
above the blanket as if trying to catch
something running away, something elusive
like a little animal, or water.
Those were the last things that he said and did.
I think of them together now with Hamlet's
fell sergeant death, so strict in his arrest,
and an old friend whose last email to me
spoke of his body suddenly shutting down.
That must be how it happens sometimes, quickly,
though in Grandad's case his words were followed
by a period of unconsciousness
and laboured breathing which at last just ended.
At the time it filled me with depression,
and an oppressive sense of pointlessness,
but now it seems *all part of life's rich pattern,*
as Mr Patel used to tell the staff room.
So does that sound nothing prepared me for
coming from his throat, only the once,
but clearly, like the hollow clatter I'd made
as a small child, rattling a pair of dice
excitedly inside a plastic tumbler,
though this noise sounded like a single die,
shaken reflectively, and not so fast.

The Oak Tree's Pulse

When I was twenty-three, my parents out,
the house and garden having an odd stillness,
I walked down to say goodbye to childhood.
I was going, though I didn't know it,
to a new life, and this place would never
quite be my home in the same way again.
I stood under the oak, beside the damson
on whose spines I'd often pricked my fingers
reaching for the tart, resistant harvest.

Consciously fanciful, I said farewell
to that spot where I had played and daydreamed,
close to the railings in between our garden
and the wilderness of the embankment
where local trains rocked to and fro all day.
From the age of three I'd sat under that oak,
picking up acorns in their bobbled cups.
On their stems they made me think of Grandad
smoking rosewood pipes packed with St Bruno.

What happened next was like the sudden shock
touching a wire you hadn't thought was live.
I felt a pulse of grieving from the oak tree,
and all the living plants surrounding it,
as if something was dying, painfully.
Was it for me or for themselves they suffered?
Perhaps it was for that personality
a couple or a family creates,
which is greater than either or any
of the people who contribute to it.
The trees had opened to my openness;
we'd nurtured something that would have to perish.

I don't know. The sadness and its force affirmed
that what was ending had been not a dream
but real and undeniable. That must be

why I can't help going back over it.
I never doubt that there was sorrowing,
as palpable as it was intangible.
Against the accommodations the mind
makes with what we do, and what we live through,
that implacable woundedness keeps me,
as much as anything can keep me, honest.

Hydrotherapy

Whenever I was on a visit to them,
if I was sitting with a book or paper
in the living room, or the dining room,
she'd come in and start talking. And go on.
I put it down to the combination
of energy and permanent discomfort
mounting to varying degrees of pain,
resulting from her polio in childhood,
that there was always something agitated
and agitating about her arrival,
something he used to refer to in his own
whimsical manner by saying to me,
as we sat in companionable silence
and heard uneven steps along the hallway,
the heaviest thump timed to coincide with
the adjective in her shouted war-cry, 'it's
a *grand* life if you don't weak-e-en,' after
her swim, open-air even in winter:
'mind your pockets.' But it was different if,
exhausted by the rigours of my job
from January to April, I lay
sunning my back on the too-short lounger
above damp grass beyond the apple tree
with my eyes closed, half awake, half sleeping.
She'd find me and begin weeding the border,
and start speaking to me while she did it.
The out-loud stream of consciousness continued
as irresistibly as it did indoors,
but with a different tone, another manner,
trickling round tomato plants and roses,
the influence of the garden working on her
so that her monologue, which needed only
a listener, me in particular perhaps,
but not an answer, was entirely soothing,
like the sound of water over pebbles,
which through my closed eyes and the warm skin

on my back I could hear and see sparkling,
and feel myself as if convalescing
under the unfailing gentle massage
of her voice, her company, her presence.

Seeing Trees

He'd told me with subdued intensity
that if he was ill – I'd known what he meant,
near the state Grandad was in, unconscious,
breathing heavily in the sofa-bed
Mum had made up in what was normally
our sitting room, with now no likelihood
of any resolution but the one –
if he was ill, he'd said, he'd like to be
where he could see trees out of the window.

When his time came he had another stroke
and I was on the other side of England.
He sat beside his bed in his dressing gown
and seemed to know, Mum said, that this was it.
They took him to the cottage hospital
Where, before I understood how bad it was,
let alone had time to go and see him,
he died that evening of pneumonia.
I don't know if there were trees within range
out of the window, or if he was conscious
and could see them. When I got home next day
Mum looked up at the ceiling, where his stick
in his last months had often banged the floor
to summon her, and with a stifled sob
said, sorry, the most eloquent one-word
poem, and I've encountered quite a few,
I ever saw performed, of course once only
and except inside me unrepeatably.

Later she said, hesitantly but with
shy hopefulness, perhaps he'll come back now
as he used to be, meaning wise and kind,
and sprightly too as she remembered him.
Shaking her head in his declining years
she'd say, they used to call him spring-heeled Jack.
Even late on, she told me more than once,

he'd come in from his usual morning walk
one day each May announcing, with an air
of understated but real exaltation,
which she caught perfectly so that I hear her
saying it, and through her, him, the way I know
he would have said it, the chestnuts are out.

Warm Work

I was not an eagle's talon in the waist
when I lifted my mother's pick above
my head and brought it down on a tree-root
she wanted rid of in her garden border.
The day was warm and I soon took my shirt off.
Someone saw me, someone watched me, someone
no longer with us told me afterwards
how she had enjoyed watching me working.
You might call my remembering it today,
so many years later, vanity, or my
articulating the memory boasting
and I wouldn't want to argue with you
but I see it differently. We don't own
the power we sometimes have over others
or the paradise of relative good health
and fitness, only coincide with them
for a period and then if not cut short
outlive them as the years soften our edges.
Seeing ourselves through other people's eyes
makes moments vivid with imagination.
I sense the warmth of the sun on my back,
fresh air on my skin, pleasure of exercise,
the gratification of finding later
I had for once seemed to somebody else
an action man and not a skinny bookworm.
I feel affection for my late admirer
and the tranquil goodness, a corrective
to any kind of self-concern or posing,
of working for my mother in her garden.

To Die For

Who thinks Josh in accounts is to *die* for,
the loud girl at the other table said,
in the intimate space of the restaurant
where there were just her group and ours, in shock,
having convened at the family home
for the first time since its last survivor
had been found lying on the kitchen floor.
We'd had more than a week to come to terms
with a reality we couldn't grasp,
each of us in our separate towns and countries.
Now we'd come face to grey, bewildered face
in the cold house where she would have fed us.
We thought that going out for a hot meal
would be some relief, and it might have let us
start to relax and talk of other subjects,
if it hadn't been for that empty vessel
trying to liven up her office party
which sounded almost as funereal
as we were by calling out a dozen times
about the various absent colleagues
she fancied, with emphasis on the key word,
who thinks Martin is to *die* for? I thought,
of course, as she went on repeating it,
to go and ask discreetly, would she mind
putting her question in some other manner,
trying, myself, to find the words to tell her
why our table would appreciate it,
but that would only have made matters worse.
Our food was disappointing anyway,
not even warm. We ate it without pleasure,
waiting for the next to *die* for, and the next.

Freehold, Leasehold

I remember when we moved in to that house,
which at first I didn't like, missing the home
we had left behind, brighter and more modern,
and I remember leaving it. In between,
all those years of life, four significant deaths.
It was only walls and windows when we came,
and was again later, as I found out
after the sudden last of those events,
when I could still visit and stay the night.
There was nothing left of what had mattered,
though the same apple tree leaned over the grass
beyond the tool-shed, and the oak tree stood
against the spiked black railings between us
and the jungle under the embankment
on top of which familiar trains rushed past
or waited for the signal arm to rise.
The front door hadn't changed, and the staircase
still curved up from the hall towards the landing.
But even the trees looked diminished somehow,
and the atmosphere of the place was gone.
Each time I went back, hoping to find it,
I felt a bruise spreading in my insides.
It was like the presences of those who'd died;
I looked for them but they weren't anywhere.

I think now they were fully occupied
in a migration. They seem to have sunk down,
gone burrowing away from their old haunts
underground, where I couldn't follow them,
till they came up, like the spirit of the house,
the spirit of the garden, inside me.
They'll stay here now, I think, cheerful, thriving,
until it's not a building but a body
I find myself saying goodbye to, thinking,
I remember arriving, how strange that was,
and how life slowly made a home of it.

Invited In

For Cathy Freeman

My daughter was invited in and saw again
the garden of the house that I grew up in
and haven't entered now for twenty years.
She sent me pictures of the apple tree,
the French windows behind it and the oak,
recognisably the same but taller.
Everything was patterns and tangles, black
branches and twigs, it was January.
There will be leaf-buds, blossom, apples,
acorns, density of foliage, sound
of the wind and rain through all the seasons.
How would I feel, what would I think, standing
again in summer in between the trees,
the apple near the house, the tall oak guarding
the frontier where the trains go rattling past?
I've made my peace with never seeing them
again except in my mind's eye, acknowledging
I can't bring back the years I lived among them,
telling myself they live on inside me,
the trees, the house, my dead, my former self.
It's the old conundrum – inner life
making bits of the outer world precious,
then moving on to light up somewhere else.
The other day I walked out in the fields
behind the house I live in now, and saw it
from that unfamiliar perspective,
and had a sense of being contradicted.
Its being part of the objective world
seemed counter to the way we live in it,
almost more in our minds than in our bodies.
As I sit inside this morning, writing,
sipping a second mug of cooling tea,
I recall that view, that odd sensation.

It was right that it was my elder daughter
who was welcomed back inside her granny's house

rather than me. It couldn't have meant more
to me than it did to her, the next evening,
after a long journey followed by eight hours
at work, and a medical appointment,
then being stuck in traffic and exhausted.
She says she knew her sanity depended
on keeping hold of the branches of those trees.

Brinsop Poplars

Slipping away from fizz and canapés
we rounded the outside of Brinsop Court
and crossed the little moat into the carpark.
There was a wall of trees in front of us,
grey poplars in a single lofty row,
so old I could not think or wish them taller,
nor sturdier, nor more gnarled or musical.
I tilted my head back and found I had to
tilt it again to see the end of them,
the swaying tips of the trees against the sky.
How the little leaves all up and down them
flashed lighter and darker green in the stiff breeze,
while their collective whisper like the swish
of water over many million stones
in a rocky cove made a peaceful roar,
a sound more quieting than any silence.
And how each filled the spaces others left,
though still with air and light round every branch.
In that wind, while the boles of the trees seemed
not to react, they must have flexed and braced
down into their roots as their tops swayed
in a co-operative, each single leaf and stem
obeying the unseen force in its own way,
but with a harmony perceptible
as tops which bent as far as rootedness
would let them one way bent back with the tension,
following examples set around them
in movement neither uniform nor random.
All the time the motion of each leaflet
solicited the eye, its voice the ear,
and though I stood more than a tree's length off
I seemed to be enclosed and taken up
into their company like a tree myself,
standing there long enough to feel I knew
what it would be like to stay forever.
Then you came back, and we rejoined the wedding.

The Lime-Tree Year

The ancient lime tree on its square of grass
surrounded by the Physic Garden, the town wall,
the pond with goldfish, the new nursery school
and the library never ceases to give.
In early summer the untattered silk
of its new leaves, curving to points and pinked,
seems to me to be enough happiness
for one person, and though holes soon appear
they only show the tree is doing its job
of playing host to vast communities.
Then come the delicate flowers and their scent.
This July I gathered these and dried them
for an infusion to drink after meals
with guests through the late summer and autumn;
there are some left for the approaching winter.
When I walk there now after thunderstorms,
after these windy days and nights, large leaves,
generously uncrumpled and unsullied,
all a softly bright amber yellow, are laid
thickly over the grass around the bole,
which towers with its great denuded limbs
increasingly disclosed, arboreal
Venus rising from the bath of summer.
It's hard to know which to prefer, the leaves
yellow or green, unfurling or at height,
or the stark beauty of the twigs and branches;
or would be, if I didn't know I don't
have to choose but can move, as the tree moves,
through all the seasons, between earth and sky.

Sharpenhoe Clappers

For John B Davis

John spreads his arms out like a noble scarecrow.
'Southwest,' he nods one way, and then, 'northeast.
So we are looking,' which we are indeed,
gazing at the plain laid out below us,
green country with occasional settlements,
and a water tower in the middle distance,
'northwest. I like to think the glacier
of the last ice age reached this far south,
but hadn't quite the energy to push
over the ridge into the next valley.'

What I like is to listen to John talking.
I'm feeling buoyed and blessed, up on this height,
by what must be the spirit of the beech wood.
The view from the centre, out across the plain,
framed by the tall spires and spindly branches
of the trees on the edges of the forest,
or of the trees themselves with that green backdrop,
is something I would like to live with daily.
In summer this place is alive with skylarks,
the slopes below teeming with butterflies.
I want to come again in any season,
but I know better than to let that thought
stop me being present in the moment.

Beech mast is thick in the leaves underfoot.
Beeches refrain from fruiting every year
to stop the numbers getting out of hand
of deer and boar, which feed on mast and acorns.
We are puzzled by green leaves deep in the wood,
forms of clematis which take advantage,
like the wild boar, beetles, and diseases,
when a family of trees is weakened
by putting out so much of its resources
into the wherewithal for reproduction,
for what the forester whose book I'm reading

calls, in the heading of the chapter quoted
by me to John about the beech mast, love.
The four of us complete our woodland circuit.
An Iron-Age fort may have crowned this hill,
or not. Now what crowns it is this beech wood.

The Golder Narrow

For Anna Freeman

This is the story of the Golder Narrow.
That's the Narrow which is more golden than
any other Narrow whatsoever.
Here is a boy with his little brother
standing under an apple tree with trains
going past the bottom of the garden.
The little brother misses his old house.
When are we going home, he asks each morning,
until he gets so tired of hearing nothing
to his liking in reply he asks instead,
am I four yet, looking for any comfort.
He won't remember the day the answer's yes,
only the hope extinguished of the no.

But that's running ahead of ourselves a bit.
He still thinks of this as temporary.
In fact it is the first time they have stood here,
he and his oracle, his fount of knowledge,
this marvel who is eleven and complete
in a way he'll never be complete himself.
His hero tells him that there is a train
pulled by a great steam locomotive
so important it has a special name,
The Golder Narrow, and that – here he spreads
his arms out and turns in a circle,
while his still not four-year-old disciple
watches and listens, hears the words forever
joined to the sight of that slow revolution –
everyone in the *wo-orld* has heard of it.
From this moment dates his understanding
of the vastness of the peopled planet,
and the way it circles on its axis.

Later the two brothers and their father
stand indoors beside the tall French windows.
The three of them are feeling the ground shake.

49

Then glass rattles in the window frame,
as if its teeth were chattering with terror.
A rumour nearly too low–pitched to hear,
beginning almost in imagination,
gets louder, higher, closer, faster, faster,
until it makes all talk impossible,
while through the leaves and branches of the oak tree
they watch the enormous engine hide the sky
followed by brown and golden Pullman coaches,
each window with a yellow lighted lampshade.
The Golder Narrow, says his father, adding,
in slow meticulous enunciation
which makes the final syllable sepulchral
and lengthens it like a note in music
to three times what might be its proper length,
La Flè-èche d'O-o-or. At not quite four
he begins acquaintance with the world
of different languages and of distant travel,
a train carrying people to a ferry
which crosses sea, met by a French train like it
to bring them to a foreign capital.

Years pass. The sound of windows rattling,
the feel of ground shaking under them
become familiar as the boys grow taller.
This is their only home, they both know that.
One day the older brother climbs the oak tree
and photographs the approaching engine
with a magnificent great golden arrow
slanting across the front of its black boiler.
The younger watches the train pass with people
sitting on either side of those bright lampshades
looking out blankly, though in his direction.
He understands that there are other worlds,
impossibly remote from his, with glamour.

As unremarked, it seems in retrospect,
as the dissolving of the dew in grass
on summer mornings, steam engines vanish.

Electric trains now make the only music, some
taking passengers from Victoria
to Dover, one of them with the old name
and the brown and yellow Pullman coaches,
but everybody knows it's an imposter.

One boy leaves home, and then the other boy.
They grow up and have children who
come to visit their grandparents here,
though the youngest of them can't remember
their grandfather, to them it's Granny's house.
The former three-year-old visits his daughter
where she lives in Marseille and notices
a poster on her door with that old name,
The Golden Arrow, pictures of two trains,
And the words, The Trans-Siberian Express.
He tells her what I've been telling you. She asks
Whether she ever saw the Golden Arrow.
He has to think about it. Sadly, no.
This conversation happens on Christmas Day.
He writes it out next day, which is the birthday
of his brother who is visiting his son,
and his son's family, in up-state New York.

2: Passport Renewal

Vee Oit

When I think of people at a distance
from any centre, I remember Mayshtree –
that's a rough English approximation
of her Bavarian name, perhaps in German
Mäshtri, but I never saw it written.
Vee oit, she asked me, which the lad my age
translated, *wie alt*, she wants to know how old.
She was bent and her face was half concealed
by the scarf she could barely see out under,
but neither her age nor her heavy clothing
interfered with how she used a scythe
to mow the wheat in that strip of the field
where the teacher's son and I were helping.
I learned to tell wheat from rye, oats, and barley
by their German names before I could have said
what sort of grass the English words referred to,
though I'd read about the bearded barley,
seen ears of wheat on packets of brown flour
and heard a phrase about sowing wild oats.
Mäshtri had lived her life in this small village.
She'd moved with the times, used fertilizer
with too heavy a hand. Günter pointed.
You see that strip over there on the slope
where the corn is all flattened, where it's lying?
That's hers. That other strip? That's hers as well.
I was invited to her house, glanced over
the half door opposite where we had entered
and saw a tranquil cow stretched out on straw.
I peered up the chimney as invited
and glimpsed blue sky above the hanging ham.
I was the sole outsider in the village,
but a couple from Bremen passed through once
and told me that they couldn't understand
the dialect any better than I could.
Mäshtri wanted to know where I was from.
London, I answered, as if that explained it.

she looked blank. Günter gestured towards the hill. Over there, he said. Further than Nuremberg.

International Incident

As I pushed the door open from the courtyard
into the school hall that was our common room
for the week straddling New Year, one young Frenchman –
we were all twenty or thereabouts – growled
to a woman sitting indecisively
at the piano, with a way he had,
knitting his unusually black eyebrows,
looking ferocious, pointing at the keyboard,
joue. Though he must have thought he was all right,
sending himself up enough to make it
acceptable, I didn't, and said, without
vehemence, and almost wearily, *fasciste*,
because it seemed appropriate to something
coercive in his nature which would out
if it ever got the chance to be itself,
without pretending to be mannerism,
a harmless little eccentricity.
The woman relaxed, stood up and walked away.

An intense young man from Bratislava,
wise with the fast-tracked awareness nurtured
by growing up in a police state, where
the word fascist was part of an armoury
of insults also including bourgeois,
capitalist, and imperialist,
happened to come in out of the courtyard
after me just in time to witness all this.
I saw him lighten up with a faint smile,
almost of relief I think, at having what
he too must have perceived articulated
with so little tact, recognizing
that whatever word I used and whether
or not it was appropriate, I'd seen
an embryonic version of a kind
of personality he knew too well.

Killing a Horsefly

We were twenty-one, and both looked younger.
We had accreditation, responsible
together for running a work camp, two weeks
with students working on the land somewhere.
We were the advance guard. It was hotter
than I was used to, or had almost ever
been exposed to, and the time I had been
seemed like another life, another person's.
So this exposure was a revelation,
punishing and delicious. I was learning
how it felt, and how I felt about it.

But the horseflies – I've never seen insects
exactly like those, either before or since.
They didn't look particularly unclean.
They were large-bodied, with their long brown wings,
when they landed to feed on someone's arm,
tucked tidily along their backs, more like
grasshoppers than anything else I knew.
In that earlier life I had been bitten
and my arm ballooned, and stayed up two days,
subsiding by itself with no harm done.
Now these creatures gave me micro-punches
if I wasn't quick enough swiping at them,
and left their marks, but nothing serious.

A sunburnt local man was talking to us.
He no longer felt any sensation,
he said, when one of these attacked him.
He showed us how he watched it as it fed,
like a fool, *comme un con,* and how when bloated
with his blood it was no longer agile.
As he talked on he swept it off his arm
with his free hand, and killed it as he did so.
How the sun kept beating down on us!

It was almost as if I had expected
the horsefly's death to turn the heating down.

He seemed to want to entertain us, tell us
his unhappy story, and I think I know
what he saw in us, and knew it at the time,
knew how it felt to be us was different
from how it seemed to him, but still enjoyed
the role he was projecting on to us.
Fresh-faced young lovers, what could be sweeter?
He'd had a very limited social life,
took his breakfast in the same café
every morning – how exotic that was
to me, breakfast in a café ever,
let alone every day! There was a girl
who had her breakfast at the same café.
So in the course of time he married her.
That was how he told it, bitterly.
Nothing else about their life, or her,
or whether they had children, other interests.

The terms hadn't been invented, but that man
was from somewhere, and though we didn't know it,
we were on course for being from everywhere,*
which in some people's minds amounts to nowhere.
His somewhere felt worse than nowhere to him,
but had compelling authenticity
for us, young outsiders, full of wonder
at how he held his sunburnt arm up, talking,
inviting us to watch the horsefly feeding.
We were his connection with the air,
with all the possibilities of flight.
He was our connection with the earth.
Through him we felt roots growing from our feet
into a nourishing, historic darkness,
a different kind of cool enfranchisement.

* Somewhere and anywhere are terms used by David Goodhart in *The Road to
Somewhere*, Hurst Publishers, London, 2017. In 2016, Theresa May had declared:
'If you believe you are a citizen of the world, you are a citizen of nowhere.'

Eh, Monsieur, Une Cigarette...

It always used to make my daughters laugh
if I suggested going for a drink
in a turn of phrase I'd learned at twenty,
on va prendre un pot? Nobody said
fancy a jar in those words any more,
just as no-one I know calls the cinema
le cinoche or an American
un Amerlo. I daren't waste their time
inquiring whether any of the expressions
I found so glamorous and picturesque
is still in use. I think the word for dosh,
le fric, still has currency though not in francs.
If we still smoked I wouldn't ask them
tu veux en griller une, do you want to grill one? –
and I'd be wary of the synonyms
in that great song from the Depression era,
un clope, une cibiche, and *un mégot.*
Clope is still fag, *mégot* still means fag-end.
Une anglaise or *une blonde* were ready-mades,
paler than the pungent and much darker shag
in *Gitanes* and *Gauloises,* or *du gris,*
the stuff the tart tells the man she's chatting up
she likes to take into her fingers and roll.
Non, point d'anglaises, ni d'bouts dorés,
goes the song, she doesn't want any of those,
and adds, *Ce tabac-là, c'est du chiqué.*
that draw's too poncy for her liking. *Du gris
que l'on prend dans ses doigts et qu'on roule.*
Why should my daughters or my grandchildren
care how we sang *chansons* in the *bagnole*
heading out to watch the latest Godard
at the *cinoche?* They might say as we said,
though they'd find another way to put it,
that they cared as much about the answer
as they cared or didn't about their first shirt,
je m'en fous comme de ma premiere liquette.

Who now would say *liquette* and not *chemise?*
As we began to say a few years later
tout ça ne nous rajeunit pas, all this
doesn't make us feel we're getting younger.

A Conversation

For the Chiaroscuro String Quartet
and the Cowbridge Music Festival

Next we have Haydn's G Minor Quartet.
It's the dialogue in the slow movement
between the cello and the violin
that sets something inside me echoing,
and for a few uncharted, eerie minutes
is the absolute justification
for coming out to hear this music live.
It's like two human souls or essences
having an exchange, deep answering deep.

When I was in my twenties I spent a night –
I honestly forget how this happened –
sleeping in a large room with three women,
each of us in separate beds, no sex
then or at any other time, but we four
had been talking eagerly all evening.
In the morning two of them said that I
and the other woman had been speaking
in our sleep in French – she was going to France
for the first time, where I'd been quite often –
her voice anxious and mine reassuring.
Neither of us believed them to begin with.
It comes back to mind tonight while hearing,
in the adagio, deep call to deep.

Held Under

There is no as if, her analyst had said.
It was, she had begun to say, as if
her mother had on purpose held her under,
a memory so shocking she'd been certain
she must have dreamed it or imagined it.
It was as if her single mother, poor,
and with two older, more vigorous daughters,
hadn't wanted her to go on living,
perhaps especially after the latest
addition to the family turned out male,
the parting gift of a collapsing marriage.
I didn't get it when her father told me
how to go about the act of congress
in order to ensure our second child
would be a boy, I was so far removed
from any frame of mind in which that mattered.
Was it what worked at the last gasp for him?
She was closer to her mum than to her dad,
but there were tensions to which I was witness.
She knew she had a muddle to sort out
inside her, and read all the latest books
about childhood development, went for years
on Wednesdays, when she didn't have to teach,
to the wise woman who enlightened her.

The day she told me what she'd half remembered,
and how she'd been cut short, I got the picture.
I thought back to all the times I'd watched her
in swimming pools, or in the sea somewhere,
doing her awkward breaststroke, head held high,
hating, she always said, to get her hair wet.

Passport Renewal

For Anna Freeman

I am almost sure it was Montpellier,
but couldn't it have been Montélimar?
I associate that name with her too,
perhaps because she was so fond of nougat.
Wherever she was born, I always thought
she can't have lived there long. The memory
she dwelt on was of playing in a garden –
that was somewhere to the east of Paris –
with her two sisters and her younger brother,
her mother's garden, climbing the pear tree
to hide when their father came to visit.
He was highly strung, emotional, cried
to their mother and slapped the children's legs.
The one bright spot of his visits was music –
he'd bring records by Piaf, Brel, and Brassens.
She and her brother sang and learned guitar.
She never spoke to me about the south,
but when we went on holiday after
the separation, for me to be with you,
as we drove down a steep road to the sea
she relaxed into that world like someone
who has come home at last. *Ah, le mimosa,*
she said, recognising yellow blossom
which was new to me and ever since has been
one of her signatures. After your email
I opened a book and read about chicks
'tumbling over each other like mimosa'.
So, together with your question, that did it.
No good thinking about anything else.
I'm nearly sure it was Montpellier.
Your uncle will know, or perhaps your sister.

Almost Worse

For Polly Poon

The way she hugs, my emigrated niece,
whom we've not seen for years, so rarely here,
with both her children or just one of them,
to see her mum, her dad and her four brothers,
is about as total as a hug can be,
and she sits next to me, pressed knee to knee,
to talk about old times and recent troubles,
after the tears that made me hold my arms out.
They're almost worse than not seeing us, she says,
these meetings with us all, crowded and brief,
knowing it will be ages till the next one.
That saying, with its shocking truth to feeling,
her bright face, her eyes swollen from crying,
the warmth of that hug, and the joy in it —
the least I can do for her is give her
this way of making that half-hour together,
if not last, stand at a different angle
to time than what passes unrecorded.

Thursday Night on the Liffey

Dublin doesn't seem especially crowded
till we get to the second terminal
becoming more thankful to have got seats
as people press on up the bus's aisle
and keep on coming and when we get off
outside the Gresham on O'Connell Street
and walk south and right down Henry Street –
Jesus, Mary, and Joseph! – here the crowds
are worse than Christmas Eve at Oxford Circus
or Istanbul as I remember it
the best thing about which was the easy way
so many people shared the public space.

This is more like Berlin. The streets are full
of fit men and women in their twenties
striding purposefully past or at you
mostly alone but none of them in doubt
about where they're going or the point
of getting there as fast as possible.
And if any of them are at all lonely
or possessed of any sort of weakness
such as gentleness or thoughtful humour
you wouldn't know it. Now I remember
from a similar shock on my last visit
how the historic, literary Dublin
seems a fantasy, a wishful construct
of the mind when you're weaving sideways
to miss people who may be born and bred
in this city but mostly have the air
of living here intensely for one year
or two or three and then moving away
to another country, or a part of Ireland
that might as well be in another country.

Later we have Italian food and wine
in an upstairs room beside the river

next to a young woman from Sao Paulo
and her good friend, a man from Latvia.

The White Bull of Renvyle

For Theodore Deppe and Henry Lyman

Henry talks to all the animals, Sheba
the dog, the Connemara pony, Barbara,
the sheep, any other dog he comes across,
even if it's running without stopping
on an urgent errand past him somewhere,
and the white bull. As far as I can see
they are all more or less unresponsive,
and none is more so than the little bull,
with thin, white fur curling over his head,
round his half-closed eyes and down-turned mouth.
We've met this enigma several times
across one gate or another, and always,
whether in a field with cows and calves
or by himself in a small enclosure,
he looks withdrawn, hidden inside himself.
I could be misinterpreting that distance,
the way he looks at you and blanks you out.
I can't help seeing it as stoicism –
perfected, deliberate insentience.

We're in mid-September, with mixed fortunes.
Today's miraculously warm and sunny.
I've read about the gales and snow and sleet
and the endless rain of November here.
It's a good place to live if you're a scholar,
can pass the dark months in imagination,
transported to some other times and places,
with just a daily outing in the weather,
or if you're Ted, an almost daily dip
right through the year to prove to yourself
you are here, you are here now, you simply are.
I thought of him yesterday, traveling
in the mind with his long poem, written
out of grieving and this daily bathing,
and then swimming from White Strand, where he swims.
The sea was cold enough to make me feel,

if anything could, entirely integrated,
all of me nowhere else but where I was.

The white bull with his fetching matted curls
can't escape in poems or in novels.
All he can do is migrate inside, inwards.
To judge by his expression there's no comfort
where he has retreated from his boredom.
He must have made a survey of his options
and reckoned that instead of, like us, striving
to be more sensitive to what's around us,
to appreciate the whole creation,
or the bits of it each of us is able
to get at least some sort of handle on,
his best bet was to shut down everything
that wasn't actually required to function,
and wait out the remainder of his sentence
in a sort of willed unconsciousness.

Maybe it's a kind of wisdom. Henry says
that in another life he was a dog.
Perhaps the bull next time will be a seeker,
the follower of a Buddhist master.
He might be luckier, miss out some stages,
and having glimpsed Nirvana in a snowstorm,
doing his best not to be while being,
get off the wheel of reincarnations,
graduate to a final emptiness,
awarded non-existence like a rosette.

The Marram Grass

For Henry Lyman

My nape ached with the cold as if somebody
had it in a vice, so did my fingers,
but I persevered, swam under water,
turned on my back and gazed at the blue sky
with small white clouds and a fading contrail.
I looked around me at the hilly islands,
and wasn't sure I was getting that fine
magical sharpening of defective eyesight
I've nearly always had in other bathings
in chilly sea on spring or autumn days.
But then I danced and sang along the sloping
smooth sand where only one small seagull
had left its tracks before me, and then Henry,
who had been swimming too, and I together
paced along the shore and talked about it,
and I spoke of feeling now accepted –
I glanced inland – by those clumps of grasses,
the marram grass growing out of the dunes,
and in the saying knew that it had happened.
I felt admitted here, an enrolled member
of some society of seaside beings.
As we walked up dry sand in warm sunshine,
with the tide coming in fast behind us,
knowing that this would probably, given
the forecast, be the last time we'd do this,
I felt what other people must feel daily
in summers on idyllic ocean beaches,
a total relaxation into something
hard to describe or name, but whose appearance
is what happens to be there at the time –
marram grass, white sand, abandoned boats –
which afterwards, if it's at all remembered
will signify a heightened state of being,
carefree, exalted, utterly included.

An Encounter in Clifden

She was all set for an elaborate trip,
and then the call came that the alcoholic,
the miserable cow who was her mother
was ill, and it meant *really* ill this time.
She was in Africa, an aid worker.
A nurse she had been working with told her,
you know you'll go, you may as well accept it.
Look after her, and if she doesn't die,
kill her. The daughter, telling us this, laughs
as her friend must have laughed, uses the phrase
gallows humour, but laughter and the label
barely domesticate the gunshot echo
of some archetype of experience
encapsulated in this stranger's story
as we sit in the school gymnasium
waiting for the concert to get started.
She didn't have, she says matter-of-factly,
a mother-daughter relationship with her.
After a lifetime of continual grumbling
she seemed at the end to grow more peaceful,
gave up resisting and was ready to go.
What she's seen, she says, has changed her mind.
Now she can't agree with euthanasia.
She earns her living as a social worker
in England, comes back to Connemara
for holidays, inherited a house here.
She couldn't sell it, there's no running water,
but she lets it, doesn't want to leave it
empty when there's such a housing shortage.
She loves to go for long hikes in the mountains.
If you lie down sometimes you can walk further.
She might have told us more, but the lights dimmed
and, after we'd clapped, the conductor lifted
his baton and the orchestra began
with the overture to *Die Fledermaus*,
a rousing, energising roller-coaster

getting us ready for the main attraction,
the international legend in his lifetime.

Tiny Incident, Salthill

We were walking back along the pavement
behind a family group after an evening
listening to live music in O'Connell's.
An eleven-year-old pushing a buggy
caught the handle of a child's bike standing
beside a café table, the bike's owner
nowhere to be seen, and the buggy-pusher,
with only one hand free, held the bike upright,
trying without success to make it stable.
I could see the lad was getting nowhere,
and heard myself say, just loudly enough
for him to hear, you need help, and as I spoke
I put my own hand on the bike, the boy moved on,
and I could see the shape of the machine,
and turned the front wheel to the proper angle
so it would stand till someone came to claim it,
or another passer-by should knock it over.
It was a satisfaction to do that.
What made it even sweeter was that thankyous
came from the boy himself and from his mother,
and a four-year-old with red curly hair
smiled at me shyly with appreciation.
It wasn't that I needed to be thanked,
but that they showed their graciousness, and made
my ten-cent good deed worth as many euros.
As we walked round the five or six of them
the mother apologised for taking space
as she schooled the little ones around her,
saying as if to everyone and no-one,
we're all over the shop, and I thought of saying,
so's everyone, don't worry, but I didn't,
thinking there was enough good will established
and present like a fragrance in the air.
Articulation of it might have spoiled
the delicacy of the moment, and now
I hold in my mind's eye with satisfaction

the shaped racing saddle of the bike,
reassuringly stabilised as I looked
and knew I had done something simple right,
seeing implicated in its elegance
the spontaneous flowering that followed.

The Cliffs of Moher

She licks the side of his face very slowly,
starting from the muzzle and working back
along under the ear, taking her time,
time during which several walkers behind me
have said ah, glancing inland but not stopping,
among the others who have passed in silence
or continued with their conversations
in a dozen languages. I watch the cow
carry on licking her calf without haste,
working backwards along the flank as if
she plans to keep on going to the tail,
and then maybe do the next layer down,
like someone painting as a meditation.

The calf has been stretching his head forward
and up, as if wanting his chin stroked or scratched,
perhaps a kind of automatic reflex.
Now he interrupts her steady progress
by turning to present his other side,
and she starts in again from the beginning.
Restless, he darts under her towards her teats,
and butts a couple of times as if he's hungry.
From where I'm standing her back legs obscure
my view, but her udder looks non-existent.
The teats are visible, but there's no bag
heavy with milk, she hasn't got any.
He's a big fellow after all, weaned surely,
and maybe she's dried up naturally,
or is suffering from some condition.
It's as if all this elaborate grooming
meant, I can't give you milk, but I love you,
and his butting her was saying, I know.

I walk on to the next viewpoint looking
down the cliffs, and out across the ocean.
People are disregarding notices,

lying flat to hold cameras and phones
over the edge. Near them other people,
some smiling and some solemn, pose for portraits.

When I pass the field on my way back
another cow, this one with milk to spare,
is being suckled by her calf. From behind me
somebody takes a photograph of that.
I see the first cow and her half-grown offspring,
not licking, not butting, still keeping close,
side by side, communing with each other.

Late August in Shop Street

I'm good, thank you, the woman answers,
after she's asked how I am and I've told her,
while I watch her wrap the marmalade
infused with Irish whiskey we have chosen
for the couple who have been kind to us
back in Wales, and she smiles a little,
just enough to oil the wheels of commerce.
I glimpsed her from a distance earlier
between customers, a fine young woman,
tall, with long dark hair, a stately manner –
when I said young, I might have said, still young –
gazing into space with an expression
of boredom, discontent, and disappointment.
It's a variant of the desolation
I've seen on many faces in this quarter
thronged with tourists under festive bunting,
enlivened by the music of the buskers,
faces of people trying to get attention
and custom or donations in the streets,
or other people standing behind counters.
It's late in a rainy summer season.
There's no novelty for anybody
working here now in their situation,
just repetition, long hours, tedium,
the knowledge that in two or three weeks' time
this gig will be well and truly over,
and whatever keeps them here, playing parts
they have grown weary of, will let them go,
to find something to do they may like less.

Getting Them In

I used to run a pub down in Bromley.
The council sent this lad wet behind the ears.
Why are those men still here at twenty past?
Didn't even know his own regulations –
they're allowed those twenty minutes to drink up.
Look, I said, I'm a human bein. It's not
just rainin out there, it's *pissin* with rain.
Those four men are waitin for it to pass.
I'm not turnin them out on a night like this.
After that I got a horrible letter
off Kent Council and then I moved up here.

The changes I've seen you wouldn't believe.
Yes, in Lewisham. In Ireland as well.
People left their doors and windows open
all day and all night. They never do that now.

The po-liss used to be all right. At Christmas
you'd give a couple of bottles of whisky
to the sergeant and a couple of bottles
of brandy to the inspector and he'd say,
if you have any trouble you call me.
Now it's councils. Always down on you, they are.

Pity you didn't come in earlier.
You missed the regulars, a man from Galway,
one from County Clare like me, one from Sligo.
You expect the man from Sligo gets fed up
with people mentioning W B Yeats
to him? I expect he does. I've no doubt
he does. I've put your drinks on the other bar.

Meeting Her Father

For Joe Allard

When Joe was, as he puts it, living in sin,
although it's not, he adds, a concept they have,
with his future wife in Japan and he was
about to meet her father the first time,
he asked how deeply he should bow. Having
her back to him at the time she answered
without thinking, thirty degrees. She turned,
saw his astonishment, laughed, and explained.
He is your elder and my father and you
are a foreigner. On the other hand
you are better educated than he is
and probably earn slightly more. Jaw dangling,
he asked her if she really calculated
all these and other things on meeting someone,
automatically graduating bows
according to instinctive computations.

An Englishman can't hope to feel at home there
is the point of the story, though Joe does,
far more than most, and plans to spend next year
teaching in Tokyo, where signs on the stations
are written in three different alphabets.
They are the most civilised people, he says.
There was no looting after the tsunami.
Yes, they have crime, an underworld, and gangsters:
in the aftermath of the disaster
it was the gangs who provided aid. He says
theirs is the least 'spiritual' of cultures.
They are brought up Shinto, but they sometimes turn
to Buddhism in times of crisis, seeking
comfort in the face of annihilation.
When I saw people joining hands in prayer,
taken to the rubble where their homes were,
that would have been Buddhist.

                         I learn a lot
from listening to Joe, and asking questions,
but the image that illuminates it all,
at least for me, is that of him, long ago,
in a room somewhere, with his new girlfriend,
she busy with her hair or some cosmetics,
having that kind of exchange people do have
when they don't need to watch each other speaking.
I feel the intimacy of that moment,
the fragrance of skin freshly-bathed, and Joe
remembering a time when youth and love
must have seemed safe from earthquakes and time passing.

3: Country Dancing

A Walk I Often Do

The advantage of a walk you often do
is that once you start you tend to go on.
I could have called it a day yesterday
being tired and the afternoon advanced,
and having driven for an hour earlier
into the glare of February sun
which was still mugging me from behind shadows
cast by buildings and trees and throwing
blindness into my eyes as if with malice.
I took one step and then another without
letting myself think further forward than that,
the way I've got through these last busy weeks
doing the next job and then the one after.
I hesitated when I had just started,
feeling my dragging weight and ruminating
about what still needed doing back at home.

Once I was climbing the slope between the trees
a little burst of joy like a kindled flame
breaking out in a sudden glow lifted me
by surprise, my muscles saying thank you
to be taxed and stretched, given something to do;
my working lungs said amen, and thanks, too,
for the sweet cold air higher up the hill.
I paused, noting the quickness of my breathing,
and looked past the new white walls shining
in the last brightness at the local landmarks.
I was into my stride now and only
the years that bring the philosophic mind
stopped me doing the walk's longer version.

I still had the pasture to cross and stopped
to look back, as I do, at the wooded hill
where the square tower of the Norman church
was silhouetted against fading sky
among the x-ray traceries of trees.

As I walked on again I saw geese resting
on the grass beyond the river where last week
I'd seen two swans, unusual visitors.
When I regained the road I heard a robin
singing in a nearby canopy, looked up,
and saw a shape that might have been a sparrow,
but there it was, just visible, the red stain.

Country Dancing

The dog-walker comes towards me squinting
and I step aside to let him pass. By way
of acknowledgement he begins to speak,
complaining he can't see against this glare.
Now we've circled each other and changed places,
so I'm the one looking towards the west.
I touch my peaked baseball-style cap. That's why
I wear this, I say. He points to the grass.
It's still white with frost where it's in shadow,
he says. I look. It is. Houses down there
must be all right, he says, they get all the sun.
There's a row of new conservatories,
all facing south beyond the flooded field.
I laugh. I wouldn't want to be in there
in a hot July. As an afterthought
I add, if we have any more hot Julys.
I'm thinking how for us global warming means,
or may mean, wetter, cooler summers, and if
nobody's certain about that, I do know
that last year when the children visited
we didn't swim in the sea a single time.
True, says the man. I see a friendly face,
a slight stoop, but a large, vigorous frame,
with a small white whippet waiting patiently.
We each turn the way that we were heading.
I'm left with the comradeship of walkers,
the sight of frost on dandelion leaves
like icing picked out on a crimped rosette,
and this sense of having performed a dance,
revolving round each other, beginning
to talk, and standing still afterwards only
as long as it would take to bow or curtsey,
before, keeping the rhythm flowing, parting.

March Colours

for Amanda Rackstraw

Look, I say to Amanda, look down there
at the anemones, the wood anemones
under the trees among the celandines.
We stop to look at them and go on talking.
There are crowds of the white star-like flowers,
and crowds of the yellow ones, just as star-like,
distinct masses of the different colours,
but with no hard borders, freely blending.
Last time I walked here talking it was with
Shelagh and Martin, and later Shelagh said
she'd been too absorbed in conversation
to take in the sights she'd looked forward to,
which is why I don't hesitate today
to interrupt whatever we are saying
to point out something to Amanda, who
probably doesn't need me to, but I
see things better for announcing them, the first
blue violets all along the roadside,
so plentiful they must have been there surely
the last time I came this way, although
this is certainly the first time I've noticed.
And look, there are a few white violets too.
Later Amanda stops and looks up, saying
what an intense blue the sky is, cloudless,
and it is, though as I choose not to mention,
there's some soft white fluff westwards behind her.
It isn't the complete absence of vapours
that matters but the blue experience,
the depth of what I glance at while she gazes.
Mine are the anemones, the sky is hers.
She asks about the march we've been on, and I see
the celandines in circles on blue backgrounds,
with lettering of white anemones.
Yes, I say, there was a lovely feeling,
upbeat, in spite of everything, like this,
she with her stick, me with my feet still aching.

Antique Land

St Quentin's castle was left uncompleted.
There never was a battle to attack
and defend it, arrows and siege engines,
no boiling oil. The keep is little more, now,
than a pile of stone. On the road side the Gatehouse
looks like a Gatehouse, a pointed stone arch
between two towers crumbling at the edges.
Did they go on building it so massive
out of habit even when they thought they knew
that war was over for ever in these parts,
and the castle would be just a residence?
There's a civil war battlefield near here –
Stalling Down, where people walk dogs and fly kites
with the buzz of unseen traffic in their ears.
I prefer this hill, further from the motors,
where no fighters killed or maimed each other.
The symbol of oppression is a ruin
as picturesque as some Gothic folly,
which in its own way, like the broken statue
of Ramses the Second in the desert sands,
makes you more optimistic about life.

Keeping A Welcome

I don't come this way on a road to nowhere
for the fun of hearing the distorted chimes
of the Mr Whippy ice cream van, playing
over and over again the first nine notes
of We'll Keep a Welcome In the Hillsides, but
there it is, butter-coloured, blocking the lane,
and there's a harmless, stooped, grey-haired woman
having a chat while she is buying something,
and here's me thinking, it must brighten her day,
no-one else calls here, perhaps she's lonely.
Though I can't see the driver properly
I get a sense of him, quiet, middle-aged,
struggling to make a living probably,
and years of indignation at this pling-plong
heard in city streets, even more denatured,
louder, played more frequently and longer,
count for nothing, my heart set against it
softens to the consistency of ice cream.
I sidle past the van and walk on down
across the ford, back up the other road,
and hear the tune again, unseen this time,
and a front door opens. Two children run out
down to their gate with their faces lifted,
open-mouthed and pointy-nosed, blinking like moles
sniffing out signals, and I can't help melting
at the sight of them, with their laughing mother
in jeans tumbling out of the house behind them,
especially as their snouts are pointing up
instead of down the street, the wrong direction,
and I call out to tell them where he is,
adding that he's coming this way, which he is,
and in so doing I realise I've changed sides,
and cheered for those to whom the ice cream jingle
is something to be glad of, not resent.
To my old self I plead in mitigation
that the volume is down, the repetitions

few and discreet. I hear the tune once more
near the end of my walk, and am able
to tell from the sound that after doing business
with those children, Mr Whippy wound uphill,
past the church, the pub, then down through the estate
of new houses, and either in to the town
or the other way, out towards Bridgend.

Exhibition

It's a cool afternoon in mid-November.
Boys are messing about beside the river,
and one of them is taking off his shirt.
Perhaps it's for a dare, or someone bet him.
I lose sight of his group among the trees
as I turn and head towards the footbridge,
but it sounds as if he must be in by now.
A dozen girls in brand-new uniforms
crowd along the path in my direction.
I notice how, whatever the colour
and the thickness of their hair, all of them
have it pulled tightly back above their foreheads.
Once you focus on it, it's a motif,
the smooth brow and the lines of hair above it.
They must be eleven, twelve at most.
Though I've lost sight of the bare-chested boy,
the girls haven't. They're pretending not to look,
not to be impressed or interested.
One of them, with dark curls, her lowered face
suffused with a becoming rosiness,
gives an involuntary, inward smile.
Who knows what is going on inside her?
I'm remembering when I was her age,
or thereabouts, and the smooth-skinned boy's,
seeing an older lad at a French resort
with a friend, no doubt egging him on,
facing a sand-dune, changing to swim, naked,
with narrow hips, flexing his small, hard buttocks,
smirking, glancing further along the beach
to where two girls, in their mid-teens as he was,
demurely dressed, holding down pleated skirts,
were sitting on a wall, giggling together,
one of them leaning back in the direction
of the sea to look past the dunes, almost
toppling, to glimpse perhaps the first male nude –
it was a different world – she'd met with, and I

didn't know which surprised and pained me more, his shamelessness, or the girl's fascination.

The Act of Being

You get the whole age range, walking between
the High Street and the children's playground, babies
in prams and pushchairs, and the elderly
leaning on sticks or wheeled out under blankets,
and you can contemplate within a minute
what it is to be five, fifteen, and fifty,
and with practice I am getting better,
I think, at running up and down the scale.
It helps that I've been coming here a while –
this man tending a toddler on a swing
I can remember as a teenager,
shy and awkward, working at a checkout.
Mostly I don't depend on recognition.
In the curly-headed three-year-old I see
the future long-legged, blushing adolescent,
in the schoolgirls, so excitable it seems
they'll leave the ground in gales of their own giggles,
the confident but slightly careworn mothers,
more muscular from all the heavy lifting.
I watch them like a time-lapse film of shoots,
having poked out of the soil and wavered upwards,
developing a swelling, then a bud,
the buds opening into flowers and fading,
the fruit forming and becoming riper.
Mother and baby, father and ten-year-old
throwing a rugby ball, family likeness
showing what one was, the other will be,
the slighter figure, the more thickset, stronger.
I run the gamut of the generations
like a piano's octaves, or from one end
of the rainbow to the other, conscious
of mysteries beyond reach of our senses,
the infrared before birth and conception,
the ultraviolet announced sometimes
by the bell tolling from the parish church.
Yesterday, turning a corner suddenly,

I saw two twelve- or thirteen-year-olds, one
forbidding her almost-twin to take a path,
with what power to compel I couldn't say,
and the other visibly reluctant
to turn back, but complying anyway,
shouting to her nemesis, I hate you.
Ah, to be so young, and so unhappy!
Part of me is all the states and ages,
and both genders, and the inbetweeners.
It's like what walking under the trees does,
pausing to smell the roses in the gardens:
I come back having been Whitmanised, vast,
more than myself, containing multitudes.

Lateral Thinking

Absurd, the way agendas weigh me down,
the way I let them, when I might be buoyant,
and float and dance through any day's surprises –
such as this spectacle, in February,
in a place that hasn't once changed colour
since last winter, of big, dizzy snowflakes,
so confused by their own wind resistance
that, though they may remember where they're heading,
they seem uncertain about how to get there.
A few of them behave as if they thought,
no, wait! I want to go back up, and others,
I'd like to see how far I can drift sideways.
Above them I make out the icy cohorts
seeming to shoot in slanting parallels,
fast, and with a single shared intention.
It's only when they get to rooftop height
they become dreamier, start to lose focus.
No wonder children love not only snow
fallen, making ice-cream cones from bushes,
carpets from lawns, and fur coats for the cars,
prompting their fingers to anticipate
the ache of turning red around small fistfuls,
but falling, as they recognize the way
their own thoughts do, urgent with purposes,
coming swiftly into view like missiles
from some mysterious source beyond them,
then slowing down and blossoming, spreading out
like opening parachutes, drifting sideways,
forgetful of all heaviness, but floating
on the sufficiency of the present tense,
each moment absolutely realized
before it settles on a leaf, or collar,
and melts, while twenty others take its place,
dancing without hurrying or ceasing.

Snow Scene

Snow is still lying, not just on the grass
but along the higher boughs and branches
of bare sycamores, ash trees, and beeches,
picking them out in picturesque designs.
I tap one horizontal iced with white.
There's not even a tremor and the sugar
stays fastened to the furrowed crust below.
Streams of white particles are shooting sideways
through gaps in hedges and off cottage roofs.
In places you can think there's a new shower
from the blue sky, but it's breeze and treetops.
Silent thrushes stalk beside the river
and on the path up under the dark trees.
Mostly the going underfoot is steady,
not dangerous, but here and there I feel
my heel slide however carefully I tread.
It may be getting worse, and certainly
the little bridge where other feet have trod
is shinier on my way back than it was
an hour earlier. I look round again
at a seemingly unpeopled world which I
and the thrushes have to ourselves, a scene
highlighted like a Brueghel, and I know
it's three o'clock on a Sunday afternoon
but it's also timeless, immemorial,
the river rushing, brimming, brown, important,
its whole chorus, basses up to trebles,
in full voice, singing its notional anthem.

Julia's Cakes

For Elizabeth Elliott

My cakes are never as light as Julia's,
she says, so sadly that I have to tell her,
you have other talents, but she answers
so does Julia, she paints watercolours,
she paints the most marvellous landscapes, portraits.
I don't like baking, she more than confesses –
affirms, a rebellious declaration.
I always feel it's such a waste of my time.
There has been a family get-together,
she says, and I think she means in the village,
knowing her son has been about, her daughter
so much in our thoughts I am not certain
whether she has been at home as well,
convalescing from her operation.
But she says it was in Kent, she likes Kent,
but doesn't know it well. It was in Deal,
on the coast, she says, and I want to ask her
to tell me more about it, the occasion
she travelled all that way for with her cake,
and what it was in Kent she saw and liked,
but conversation falters and veers off.
She looks cold, I notice, standing with me
in the car park where to my surprise,
and hers, I've come face to face with her,
busy at the open boot of the car
in the space next to mine, putting in
the last things or the only things she's bought.
I take away the picture of her sitting
on trains from Wales to London and then out,
and in between getting from Paddington
to what, St Pancras, surely, on the Circle,
carrying as I imagine it, as well
as a bag with a few necessary things,
ceremoniously, a large, round tin,
through the underworld like a talisman,
the focus of an ancient ritual,

filled with all kinds of aching heaviness,
family love, family distances,
the self-reproach of not being able
to bake a cake as light as Julia's,
but also the reluctance overcome,
and flour, and butter, eggs, and jam, and sugar.

Shaggy Dog Story

For Julia and Phil Pearson

When I sit in Phil and Julia's kitchen
Shrimp arrives, quietly padding around.
Julia always says the same two things:
she does like men. She's a terrible flirt.
Now she adds: she's very old. Shrimp pushes
her nose towards my flies gently, just once,
and then looks soulfully into my face,
and I gaze back, relaxing into the depth
of her brown eyes, their utter gentleness.
I rest both hands on her back through the long,
curly black wool of her coat. It reminds me
of a rug in my grandmother's guest room
which I slept in once when I was very small.
Julia has given me her own soft chair,
the most comfortable chair in the whole world.
She, like me, is tired, and I ought to protest.
I don't. From the other end of the table
Phil is telling me about a neighbour
who lived in the village before we came,
anecdotes that seem about to finish
but never do, opening into others.
There is no reason they should ever end.
I go on stroking Shrimp, resting my hands
on her warmth, which goes on resting under them.
I lean back in Julia's chair, waiting
for the coffee she has made me to cool,
and sip it slowly, making the moment last.

Duncan and the Kingcups

We've come to watch the new life in the pond
and visit Duncan in his garden stable.
The tadpoles are a patch of troubled water
we can't get near to without wellingtons.
I catch a glimpse of two black, moving commas,
but that's all, and I don't see any newts.
As for Duncan, he's lying in the field
sunning himself and will not come when called.
He moves his head just enough to make clear
he is sentient and must have heard us.
I had forgotten he was so enormous –
usually I've seen him close to, big indeed,
but without this perspective, and so white –
in the sun the whiteness is resplendent.
He's beautiful, showing his shapely back
as complacently as the Rokeby Venus,
which I have known since my astonished boyhood,
but I notice his has on me, given
that it's so new, such a revelation,
and that he's really there in three dimensions
and, being large, seems closer than he is,
an effect not only more entirely
aesthetic, without other complications,
but for the moment greater and more joyful.
And yet Duncan has to share the first place
in my sense of privilege this morning
with the yellow flowers at the pond's edge,
which I have never properly seen before –
though I have used both names Julia gives them –
kingcups, marsh marigolds, as like buttercups
as Duncan is like other horses, bigger,
more sumptuous and brighter, with no loss
of delicacy and charm. I'm in heaven.

Horse Sense

For Louise Oliver

I like to think horses and cows in fields
are doing all the time what I do only
for minutes here and there, as when
trying to sleep after waking at night:
sense carefully each limb, first all
the outside surfaces, and then the pulse,
the warmth and weight, the bone and muscle.
I learn the shape I am alive inside.
If I could keep this consciousness all day
I think I'd become wiser and better, not
making sudden mistakes, doing things
and thinking thoughts that don't arise
out of the totality of what I am.
I'd be like a horse, or like a cow.
I don't stay with this knowledge long enough
that they inhabit undistractedly.
Even the sheep have something to teach.
They stand in the field all day, all night.
I like to think everything their senses
brings them from inside their bodies and outside
is registered together, and in full,
while their awareness floats on all of it,
an open lily on the living water.

Living with Clouds

For Paul Ashton

Though I am glad to have blue sky as well,
I am sorry for people who don't live with clouds.
You won't believe it, said Joyce in Trieste,
but what I miss of Ireland is the weather.
Here in South Wales we've not had, this summer,
many soft days, but the clouds go on changing,
impossibly high up, with chiselled outlines,
surfaces reflecting and refracting
in ways that liberate a range of colours,
looking as if only a miracle
can keep them levitating steadily,
since anyone can see they're limestone, granite.
At other times an amnesia of grey
stretches into the distance, without feature.
Today a dreamy, soft, white airiness,
nebulous, lighter than cotton wool or silk,
is fading in and out of eggshell blue,
as a boy given to reverie drifts
into and out of all the noise around him.

If I lived where the sky is clear all day
I wouldn't miss the clouds I hardly knew.
I'd find something other than sculptured vapour,
solid, yielding, voluminous and lofty,
to compare any living consciousness
in tranquil morning meditation to,
full of percepts, concepts, recollections,
before the day comes barging in with business
to blow the clouds elsewhere, or into pieces,
or freeze them into icy arrow-heads
which spear down slantwise, gathering momentum,
swelling streams and rivers, singing, laughing,
finding their way deep into the rocks
and to the sea before finally rising
almost invisibly but copiously
until they concentrate themselves like thinking

and process, in all their laundered glory,
steadily from horizon to horizon.

Chaffinches on Cherhill Down

The only way up was a sunken path,
but there in front of us a bird was making
what seemed a desperate attempt at something,
as if trying to fly but not succeeding.
Then we stood still and got a fuller picture.
Facing the familiar livery
with its warm, bright, contrasting colours, stood
a friend in a less loud, subtler outfit,
her feet planted, her head thrown up, and her tail
just as noticeably thrust out and raised.
She was watching him, standing foursquare,
and he maintained eye contact while he danced –
as we saw now, though we scarcely believed
what we were seeing, and had never heard of –
with steps too quick to follow but so patterned
and neat we knew there was no faltering,
no inaccuracy or hesitation.
A dozen to the right, twelve to the left,
all this just a few human feet from us,
as if they were too thoroughly absorbed
to notice or, I'd rather think, not minding,
knowing that we were no kind of danger.
Next, he flew up till he was behind her,
and with his wings still fluttering, balancing,
lingered there for several seconds, until,
when we'd absorbed their paired profiles, hers passive,
braced, welcoming, his sure and balletic,
instead of going straight for consummation
he flew back to his former place, so now
they faced each other, beak to warbling beak –
he was singing loudly, she answering
with a continuous but lighter treble –
and he did his intricate dance again,
and then flew up again, and once more lingered
only a little while, miming the coupling,
and made as if to tap-dance a third time,

but something startled them – we hadn't moved –
and they exploded upwards, disappearing
in a blink beyond the hawthorn hedgerow.

A Country Church in August

In the middle of the tiled floor of the porch
a double sheet of newspaper surprised us,
its tidy print spattered with black and white
like a collage or an action painting.
The penny dropped, as it had to. We looked up,
and there in an angle of the rafters
was a miniature lined hanging basket.
All along the brim, instead of heart's ease,
petunias, or lobelia were heads,
gently simmering squash balls in the gloom.
We would have tiptoed past, as we did later,
to try the door, step inside, look around,
drink in the atmosphere, and find the Bible
opening on promises to prophets
and disciples of life everlasting.
What happened next came and went so quickly
it might have been an angel's visitation,
leaving, as only evidence, singed air.
The little round heads opened what had been
till then scarcely noticeable beaks, so wide
they showed a row of perfect amber circles,
with triangles below them and above them.
They had seen or sensed, just before we did,
the enormous parent bird with its forked tail,
exaggerated like a Beardsley drawing,
matched by wings just as extravagant,
swooping in out of nowhere at the double.
It plunged its beak into an open gullet
at the end of the row and shot off again.
Still four more hungry mouths up there to fill
and then that first one would again be famished.
I never saw such speed and elegance,
nor greater urgency and sense of purpose.
How many of the nestlings will survive?
We slipped into the church and felt the stillness,

lingered over memorial inscriptions,
and read the hopeful lessons on the lectern.

Everything's Fine

For Robert Meredith

Robert's perennially youthful face
looks more deeply lined today than usual
as we stand talking at a social distance
in the spring sunshine after he's reached out
a gloved hand with a package and I've stretched
across the void to grasp the other side.
Answering a question I haven't asked
he says, fine, everything's fine, no worries.

It wasn't fine at all at the beginning.
They weren't being given gloves or masks or space.
Things have settled down now, he tells me. But –
he grins and shakes his head. There's one bright lad
who doesn't like to be told what to do
by anybody. Royal Mail have said
we have to keep the aisles clear, but this guy
parks his trolley in the middle of one.
It stops the rest of us from passing freely.
I told him it was against regulations,
Robert says, but he was just abusive.

Next time I passed that way I shook my head,
he says, and he shakes it again now, laughing,
and this chap said to me, what's *that* about,
and I said – here his eyebrows rise towards
his neat quiff – nothing, and just kept on going.
Most people at work are sensible, he says.

Remembering my years of servitude
I say, I expect the rest of you feel
more friendly and united now there's someone
who's a pain you all have to put up with,
and Robert says, well, I've got two more years.
I'll have had enough by then. This from a man
who's always said how he enjoys his job.
He could have retired earlier, chose not to.

I've cleared and cleaned the space in the shared garden,
he says, behind the block of flats I live in,
pulled out the furniture and washed it down.
I'm on holiday the week after the next,
and I'll do what I'd do in Tenerife,
have a late breakfast, go for a long walk,
sit in the garden, have a jar or two.
There are great walks in the woods round our way,
lovely views of the valley from the garden.

I hope it'll be fine, I say, afraid
it won't be. I'll be checking the forecasts.
He turns his thoughts back to his awkward colleague,
shakes his head again. I say, there's always one.
He lightens up, repeats what I just said,
laughs, says goodbye and runs off to my neighbour.

Seeing Robert

I'd been worried that he might not have found
the weather warm enough in his time off
spent in Brynna instead of Tenerife,
thinking of him when the keen easterlies
belied the invitation of the brightness.
At least we haven't had a drop of rain.
But no, he says, he had a lovely week.
He got up early – can't stay in bed late,
thirty years as a postman have seen to that –
went for a walk, then sat out in the garden.
He gestures to the viburnum next to us.
He says their garden has a hedge that high
all the way round, with benches in alcoves.
He could sit there all day out of the wind
and in the sun from noon till eight o'clock.

It took him a few days to cut the grass,
he says, so it must be quite extensive.
I knew he'd been putting the place to rights
at weekends for a month or so beforehand.
I wonder why it all falls to him. Clearly
he doesn't mind, gets a satisfaction.
He had a drink or two in the afternoons,
went in to eat his evening meal, came back,
and sat out again until the sun set.
The way he smiles telling me this I see him
as the picture of sublime contentment.

We hear a buzz. I say the Queen would tell him
to take it, it might be important. He grins,
fishes inside his pillar-box-red jacket,
finds the phone, presses, says hello, listens,
says, can I call you back in two minutes,
I'm with a customer. That must mean me,
I think, but hey, we're mates, aren't we? As if
hearing my thought he says, that was my boss.

Oh, I think, I don't mind being that to him.
He's a whizz with computers, Robert says,
but fair play, he understands people as well,
and I say, someone wrote a book about
seven types of intelligence to which
somebody else responded, only seven?

He's got something on his mind. He stands there,
a good two metres distant so I see him
all round, four-square, energetic, bare-kneed,
his understated Elvis quiff as always
immaculately lacquered, neat and shiny.
It's like when I used to play sports, he says –
I knew he'd been captain of the Brynna
football team, but he must mean other games
as well as that which I don't know about –
what I say is, learn the basics. I gather
he's saying his boss has got the basics right,
a compliment from someone who's not always
been uncritical of the hierarchy.

Learn the basics, he says again, standing there.
That's what I've always tried to do myself.
I'm not perfect, he says. I laugh, but you are,
and he laughs with me, loosens his stance, still
standing there so I see him very clearly,
and I say, to us you are perfect, Robert,
and we're both still laughing as he turns, half walks,
half runs back to his van, his usual gait.
Under cover of mockery I've slipped in
a statement of what would embarrass him
if said too seriously, but I mean it.

Canada Geese at Evening

It's often twilight when I step outside,
and almost always I hear the geese honking
as they fly, for their own mysterious reasons,
from where they spend the day to where they sleep.
I hardly ever see them when I hear them
so I was pleased last night, having looked up
to admire the pale gold crescent of the moon
in the washed purity of a still-pale blue,
to see two geese, each sounding its wild note,
resonant and expressive and repeated.
Their necks seemed to be straining, straining forward
as if they couldn't get home fast enough,
or as if like horses pulling wagons
they felt the weight of their own bodies dragging
around invisible collars, though their wings
were stretched out wide and surely bore them up,
slowly beating against the same blue sky
from which the brightening moon looked down at them.
They flew in parallel and close together,
just far enough apart not to get tangled,
evidently in perfect understanding.
What a fine thing it must be to be one
of a pair of geese flying home at evening,
the grace of flight and yet the earnest straining,
the wholehearted effort of their reaching
reflected in their hoarse and haunting honking.

This Will Be the Day

You saw it before I did, and another,
but at least I had a good look myself
at that first swallow of the summer here
above these deep lanes around the village,
weaving elegant circles overhead
as we walked downhill between the hedges
covered in glory in the shape of leaves,
broad fans of sycamore, so that we see
mainly between them now into the fields
where there are gates, and much more rarely
than last week through them or above them.

Yes, I'm looking at you, you said, as you stood
looking over one of these gates. When I came
to where you were I saw the dapple pony
with a mane like a tousle-headed urchin
and an engaging sullen-seeming shyness.
And then, look! you said, and I did look, up,
and there it was, flying quite low, and so
appearing as it does when seen at best,
extravagantly stylised, curved and pointed.
The natural world is like a lexicon
of all the styles of art from Altamira
to Modigliani via Giotto,
the mannerist elongation of Pontormo,
and the bold lines of Beardsley and Lautrec.
We walked on through the insect-laden air.
The swallows have some catching up to do,
delayed and decimated by a storm in Greece
which laid waste to flocks of them heading north
to feast on what's been hatching from our dampness.

We admired the stitchwort, the cow parsley,
the violets and bluebells, the archangels,
even the dandelions, good friends to bees,

which all stood still for us to contemplate.
But this will be the day we saw the swallow.

—

Moth Concerto

Last thing before locking up for the night
I walk down past the open gate to the verge.
The thunder has been followed by soft rain
half inclined to identify as mist.
Now there's fragrance and humidity.
The summer solstice is only days away.
The sky's no darker than it was at seven
when we ate by the light of a tall candle,
so bright it made the sky outside seem black.
Now I look up and can't see cloud shapes, only
a soft dullness, with no stars and no moon.
On the verge as I turn to go back in
I see the moon daisies, ox-eye daisies,
gathering the light to themselves, seeming
to give it out, like the mass of deep red roses
outside the kitchen window which never fail.
On one of the daisies I see fluttering
the broad wings of a moth, diaphanous,
tremulous, shimmering, as if pretending
to be a trick of the uncertain light,
no more than a ghostly emanation.
Perhaps it's feeding on the daisy's nectar.
Inwardly applauding, I watch the mute
arpeggios of its moth cadenza,
the one thing moving till I move myself,
slowly and dreamily, up to the house.

Woodland Walk

This isn't woodland really, it's a path
overhung by trees, but it feels to me
as if I'm in a wood, with underpinnings
exposed where the brown bank has eroded.
The path is so much lower than the field
beyond the line of trees that these great roots
are at eye level, natural sculptures,
full of satisfying intricacies,
undoubtedly the product of long process,
so that just to be glancing at them slows
the speediness of modern consciousness.

It looks like coppicing, the way some stems
shoot up out of this trunk leaning sideways,
but it must be the natural consequence
of slippage having knocked the tree off balance.
It's come to terms since with its different angles,
like the others, and season after season
they've settled down to share the space together
and stop the high brown bank from crumbling further.

Hoof-prints in the mud are full of water,
but I step round them in shoes good enough
to keep my feet dry, though I'm reconciled
to the chance of their failing as the wet
from surrounding vegetation penetrates
these ragged trousers I've changed into specially.
There's lime and hawthorn, beech and sycamore.
I marvel at the gloss on the dark holly,
delicate ash leaflets against sky.
All the distances are misty, drizzle
having fallen steadily all day. It's a long path,
winding, rising, overarched with branches,
until I see the fingerpost ahead
pointing in three directions.

One of these
I took before and came to a dead end,
so I turn left, not right, and am no longer
among trees but in chest-high bracken, the path
through it so narrow that my legs become
wetter still, but I scarcely notice, mesmerised
by masses of magenta flowers, as if
I'd never seen, never appreciated
before, rosebay willowherb, head high,
larger than life, newly washed, vibrating
with energy which is also calming.
No doubt the long walk up through trees
has put me in the proper state to see them.
When people thought to build churches with naves,
did they remember walks through avenues
which had made their spirits more receptive?
I'm ready to receive communion.

I come out onto a deserted road
which leads on to another road almost
as deserted and walk downhill, seeing
the village I live in with its fields and horses,
its trees and farms, houses and gardens, spread
below me as if asking me to open
my hand over it, pronounce a blessing.

Putting Away the Parasol

We are held as if inside a bubble
by the gradual changes of the seasons,
just too slow for us to be astonished
at for example now, in late September,
being able to enjoy the sunshine
so much we sit longer out here reading
than we had intended, leaving on hold
without having to speak of it our plans
to do things which will still need to be done
later today, or perhaps tomorrow.
How many more occasions will there be
like this, before the cold and dark set in?
In July it would have been too hot
except under the parasol which today,
after it has leaned long enough inside
the back door on to the garden, you have stowed
in the garage, zipped-up, spider-free.
The subtle power of this gentle warmth
is like a more than human love and blessing.
I turn the pages of my birthday novel.
Sometimes it's almost too hot, almost too cool
when a light breeze is shifting air about.
I'm so unused to reading for this long
I have to quell a certain restlessness.
The sun is moving past the neighbours' trees.
Soon this whole area will be in shadow.
If I could suddenly be transported
to this moment from mid-January
I'd not believe it, put my book aside
to register my physical sensations.
Even now I pause from time to time
to be inside my lucky sun-warmed body.
Good to be here. I start another chapter.

4: A Sky Reflected

A Posy of Daisies in Sunday Meadow

For Don and Mary Calway

Her name has given Peter Blake his cue,
painting her portrait, in his comprehensive
depiction of all the characters from
Llareggub in *Under Milk Wood*: Bessie
Bighead. He's given her a forehead
that bulges from the level of her glasses
up to the hairline so she looks like, I think,
Hugh MacDiarmid, Trotsky, or someone else –
which other man does she remind me of?
It's like that with a lot of these portraits,
and only when I've thought this for some time
do I learn that it was deliberate:
the second narrator's Humphrey Bogart,
with different hair, added moustache and beard.
I'd thought it was Albert Camus, which shows
how alike the two chain-smoking icons were.

The one that gave the game away for me,
so there could be no doubt, was Liz Taylor.
I'd not have guessed the face with woman's hair
was Terry Wogan's. Oh yes, James Joyce –
that was the other fellow Bessie Bighead
bears a likeness to, round glasses, that expanse
of brow under the slicked-back hair. Her picture
seems done with more elaborate care
than any other, like a palimpsest
of autumn leaves, transparent, one on one,
the living eye visible behind the lens
of the spectacles like Jimmy Joyce's.

The pathos of the dream kiss for one dead,
who had kissed her once when she wasn't looking
and never kissed her again though she, you know
the rest, but there's no punch line here, only
the poignancy of lifelong loneliness.
Was the painter right to depict her and him

as their lips close in for that second kiss
older, as she is now, dreaming of him,
and as he would have been if he had lived,
rather than as they would have surely been
in her dream, young, as they had both been once?
I doubted it, but now I'm sure he was.
The youthful selves are implied, implicated,
folded in, as the layers of sepia
fold on each other in this textured painting
which makes, as all the greatest art does,
something fulfilling out of unfulfillment.

Paul Nash at Tate Britain

No question which image comes back to me first
and most clearly from the thousands we saw
yesterday on and off walls, framed and unframed:
the pale simplified outline of a grove
of winter trees with bushy canopies
on a hill with other hills beyond it.
It's a famous picture I'd seen reproduced,
one reason why it was like coming home
to see it in the third room of the show
after the mystical landscapes, night scenes
with a muse figure where the moon might be,
the often-painted elms he called The Three.
And then the blasted tree stumps of the war,
the shattered idyll of *Spring in the Trenches*,
and the reminiscence of Poussin's landscape
with a dead man in the shadows and a snake
in the monumental epic, *Menin Road*.
Next, the geometric post-war paintings
of dreary concrete Dymchurch sea-defences
in which he worked his breakdown out, and here
three or four paintings not unlike - though not
so you'd confuse them - Eric Ravilious.
Nash began as a devotee of Blake.
You might call these rare country idylls
the Innocence beyond Experience,
the inviting landscape seen from the yard
Behind the Inn, another wooded hillside,
this with autumn colours, and that more austere
but just as certainly affirmative
statement of the tall trees on a hill,
with new maturity rediscovering
that youthful feeling of the genius
of the place, and of the trees that guard it.

2

Only someone who'd survived the trenches,
if anyone, and perhaps nobody,
could be said to have earned the right to say,
as Richard Aldington – of the Artists' Rifles,
like Nash and Edward Thomas – wrote in lines
Nash illustrated in *Images of War*,
that the worst thing about the fighting was
what it did to the minds of soldiers, how it
'scattered into dust the bright wings of Psyche'.
Worst thing or not, it fits the exhibition,
and everything we know about the war:
shellshock, post-traumatic stress disorder,
at best never totally got over,
people on the home front not exempt,
such as Winifred Knights, who in Streatham
suffered some of the first aerial bombing.

3

She went to live on a farm in Worcestershire,
painted people with apples climbing ladders
to store them in an open-sided barn,
with a river and oast houses beyond it,
and herself and her cousins with potatoes
they were collecting to be stored in clamps,
a post-apocalyptic rural idyll
like Nash's sacred grove on rising ground.
For both artists, as no doubt for many
of the people at large they painted for,
it was a peak of gladness and fruition,
but they couldn't stay there. Perhaps that's part
of the meaning of that view of rolling hills:
you can go up them, but you must come down.

4

Knights had still to paint her Armageddon,
the war allegorised as *The Deluge*
about to overwhelm a fleeing people.
Then at the British School in Rome she used
the spacious courtyard of that institution
and the fellowship of its refectory
with trees from the nearby Borghese Gardens
as models for a grand *Marriage at Cana*,
with the guests, and bridal couple, and Jesus,
graceful, expressionless, hieratic,
the solemnity of a resurrection.
Piero would have been proud of her, and Lutyens.

5

As for Nash, he needed to move on. He found
nature by itself no longer enough.
Out-of-place large objects in landscapes,
interiors with views of city billboards,
these preoccupied him, international
modernism, the abstract, the surreal.
The example of de Chirico was fruitful.
A waste of scrap from German aeroplanes
he called *Totes Meer*, echoing the bleakness
of the blasted trees of Flanders and the mud.
The vision of a tall *Wood on the Downs*
was a bivouac Nash had to abandon.
Artists must always think it's their next work,
not anything they have achieved already,
which will be their best and will arrive at
what all this time they have evolved towards.

6

But we don't have to wear the painter's blinkers.
We can say, this was the summit of his vision.
In dark, uncertain times, nine decades later,
it still presents an image of endurance.
Looking at those beeches painting the sky
and joining the land to it, the spectator
feels her backbone straighten like a trunk,
her spirit open like the canopy.

Two Moments

Strolling across the square with its tall trees
and green spaces, seeing Hotel Russell,
its terracotta façade scribbled over
by the delicate hanging winter branches,
was certainly a moment of convergence –
impressions, feelings, and activities
coming together in a crystal focus.
But the pivot of the day was earlier,
sitting outside in spite of a keen wind,
eating the sandwich I had taken with me,
and drinking coffee from a cardboard mug.
One museum behind me, one ahead,
journeys on the Bakerloo, Victoria,
and Piccadilly lines to cross the city,
and walks between the stations and great buildings,
dodging traffic, seeing vivid faces,
while the plane trees and the double-deckers
sang to me of my childhood, teens, and twenties
in the siren voices of nostalgia.
There I sat, having done what I'd come for
all the morning, and lashed to the instant
by the sharp easterly I sheltered from
imperfectly behind the café kiosk,
the one customer at the picnic tables,
relishing the hot, delicious coffee.
I was being there, between two moments
about a fulcrum, morning and afternoon,
Lee Miller's photographs from World War Two,
which I had found engrossing for three hours
but for the time had utterly forgotten,
and what I did not try to look ahead to,
an exhibition, bound to be instructive,
about the history of faiths in Egypt,
with an unplanned and delightful sorbet
to end the day on, watercolours of Rome

by Francis Towne, whom I'd never heard of –
if ever I was present, that was when.

At Greenwich

For Michael Freeman

Standing next to the Observatory
you look down on the colonnades and domes
of Sir Christopher Wren's Hospital, now
part of the university, and if you know
where to look, along there far to the left,
if you stand in the one right spot, half-hidden,
seeming almost insignificant among
the taller, modern business buildings, such as
the Gherkin, with the Shard further off, St Paul's.
In front of Wren's white, elegant Hospital
is Inigo Jones's Queen's House, white too,
as gracious in a different idiom.

Dwarfing these relics of the past, behind them,
are the skyscrapers of Canary Wharf.
They make the prospect mainly vertical.
But they are so incongruous, so out
of style as well as out of scale, it is not
too difficult to think them all away,
though it works only while you pay attention.
Then you see the city, horizontal,
with a noble stretch of the broad river
winding between Greenwich and the City.
In the distance, St Paul's crowns Ludgate Hill,
reaching heavenward. Miraculously
and famously, it survived the Blitz intact.
Canaletto painted from here the London
of his day, spread out on a wide canvas.
From not far away John Constable arranged
Somerset House, river, St Paul's, cloudy sky.

While you go on thinking away those new
gigantic interlopers, as if raising
a hand against the glare of a lamp, it seems
an image of humanity reconciled,
even in one of its densest centres,

with the planet on which we have arisen,
and which many of us love so deeply.
Something inside us dilates and finds peace.
Then we relax, prepare to turn away,
leaving the teenagers taking selfies
and pictures of each other smiling sweetly,
probably obscuring Jones and Wren,
but not those towering obscenities.

At Wentworth Place

The smallness of the space and its proportions,
which feel right, like the golden mean and section,
must be contributory to the effect.
Lying in bed, before and after seeing
the colour of the arterial blood
he had coughed up and asked Brown for a candle
to be sure of, and told him he could not be
deceived in it, it was his death-warrant,
he saw the door at the bed's foot on the left
and the single large window on the right,
just as he was to when he got to Rome
and spent his last months in a room like this one,
though less well lit, and with a higher ceiling,
and with, instead of trees beyond the window,
the murmur even in 1821
of passers up and down, and people sitting,
perhaps, as they do now on the Spanish Steps,
a sound not unlike that of the fountain
which, when human noise is stilled, still rises
from the Piazza di Spagna, Bernini's
Fontana della Barcaccia, and soothed him,
prompting him to compose his epitaph:
Here lies One whose Name was writ in Water.
Despite those differences between the rooms
I wonder if their similar dimensions
as well as having held, asleep and waking,
the same inhabitant at different stages
of his vibrant life, and final illness,
contribute to my feeling, in both places,
something powerful and unexpected
I have not found the like of anywhere,
even in the most secret country churches,
except in these two rooms with half of Europe
between them, and in my case with decades
between my visits to them, so I am struck,
made momentarily almost breathless

by finding it again, this atmosphere,
arresting, charged, an absence like a presence.

Green Park Station

I have my back to the doors but they are close behind me and I press forward, pushing you into the people in front of you. I bow my head so that my outline will be inside the line of the doors where it curves at the top. I hear a woman next to me, facing the other way, saying calmly to someone behind me, it's full, wait for the next one. I half expect to hear a rebellious reply or feel a push at my back, but there is nothing, and the doors close and yes, my head is well inside the line of them. I look down into the intimate space between me and the other bodies, everyone avoiding eye contact. The train slowly starts to move, quietly, so that you can hear that nobody is talking until someone says, as if thinking aloud for all of us, this train is too crowded.

Later I reread one of the poems by Rilke in which he reflects on how much of the air around him, near and far, has passed in and out of him. It has been, as he puts it, the rind and curve and leaf of his words. Do you recognize me, air, he says, still full of places once mine? And though as I read him I am in a hotel room, not palatial but big enough, with only one other person, in imagination I am back looking towards the obscured floor as the train picks up speed, pressed in on all sides and knowing that the density of the crush stretches through the carriage, thinking of how much exhaled breath is concentrated here, how much we are recycling what has been in and out of each other's bodies.

In a way, though I don't want to repeat it more often than I can help, it makes me feel hopeful, that we can do this on a December evening in London without obvious and lasting ill effects. There is something almost sacramental about this sharing. We are so diverse, so rigorously separate, but we take the pressure of each other's flesh and we pass between us without comment what keeps us all alive, 'breath, you invisible poem': something more intimate than the skin and body hair on show in the breathless drawings of Klimt and Schiele, which some of us were inspecting half an hour earlier, two storeys above ground, in a place that seemed crowded at the time, ten minutes' walk up Piccadilly from the station where we took the escalator down to this other world.

A Sky Reflected

If I hadn't had that pint in Kennedy's
after our visit to Bloom's chemist, Sweny's,
where P J hosts readings from *Ulysses*
and crosses the road to drink with visitors,
on top of the half, and the red wine later,
I might not have lain awake till after three,
and passed the time by fixing in my mind
what I'd gazed at before lunch, and again
afterwards, in the Hugh Lane Gallery,
the single painting by Berthe Morisot
of two young women in a boat, one watching
three ducks in the water, and the other
looking straight at the beholder of the picture,
with such a vulnerable expression
she seems completely there in front of you,
affirming by her delicate openness
what it is to be properly alive,
responsive to the world and capable
of being hurt but, by the same token,
able to be moved to sympathy,
and to delight, and non-judgmental wonder.
What other painter could have caught that look?
There's something almost weak, almost unformed
about it, which makes it the more human.

No reproduction could convey its life,
I think, certainly not this postcard that I bought
anyway to remind me what it's lacking,
which is why if I could take away just one
of these great paintings – the Renoir umbrellas,
the Manet portrait or, second choice, bearing
unreproducability in mind,
the Pissarro figure in a landscape –
it would have to be this one. Every time
I strayed back in the gallery to see it,
or have looked at it since with my mind's eye,

I've had a different sense of what it is
that makes this composition so enchanting:
the girl's face on the left, certainly, but then
the touches of red, so slight you could miss them,
the trees and sky reflected in the water,
the subtle broken greens, darker and lighter,
merging with blues as the attention travels,
where the lake reflects what must be unseen cloud.
I find one small and unobtrusive passage
of paleness tinged with blue that seems to bring
the sky down like a liberating presence,
a promise of freedom from all the constraints
on these corseted girls in bourgeois Paris,
a harmony of nature with conventions
which the pale questing face of the young girl
must after all be longing for a glimpse of,
and which in the vision of Morisot,
unlike in that of her brother-in-law,
collaborator, friend, and portraitist,
Edouard Manet, is not beyond attainment.

Monet at Howth Head

For Linda Saunders

Rounding an outcrop on the coastal path
with a sudden view towards a jutting cliff,
its rugged surface midnight-blue and purple
against the ultramarine and turquoise sea,
we think of Monet. The sharpness of the light
brings what is distant close, while making clear
how far away it is, the sparkling turf
on the clifftop adding its vivid green,
while the clouds borrow colours from the gulls
and razor-bills against the egg-shell sky,
and far below a court of cormorants
in sable gowns confers on jagged rocks.

Monet would have loved all these perspectives.
He would have set his easel up and looked
and painted, painted and looked, responsive
to every change of light and to the rhythms
of day and season yet outside of time.
Surely he grew in inward sympathy
with what he saw the longer he sat painting,
or stood, and stood back, and then darted forward,
becoming every moment more absorbed
into the scene with all its sound and movement,
the feel of moving air, sweetness of in-breath,
the birds, singly and in groups, skimming the sea
or wheeling up in circles overhead.
Touching and retouching his creation,
he knew it couldn't be, shouldn't try to be,
an imitation, or the reproduction
of what anybody might have noticed.
There was no single, flat, objective image.
Hand and eye worked ceaselessly together.

We see these cliffs, these colours, and this sea,
this sky which plunges down and rises up,
the way we do because we've looked at Monet,

who never came to any part of Ireland,
but painted scenes like this in Normandy,
in Brittany, and in the south of France.
What happened through his vigils *en plein air*
was that he fashioned a new way of seeing
which his inheritors have learned from him,
spending hours over the years standing, not
at Pourville, Etretat, or Cap d'Antibes,
but in front of pictures in museums.

As we stroll back along a white dust road
stretching into the distance, scattered walkers
receding to a vanishing point ahead,
with gorse and heather blooming on all sides,
I say, Pissarro has been here before us.

Talking Books

I'm reading Darwin's *Origin of Species*
with my ears, not minding the slow traffic
if it lets me finish another chapter.
I didn't think it would be so absorbing.
It's full of marvellous details about ants,
sweet peas, pigeons, bees and mathematicians,
and visionary in its implications,
accumulating in the way great chords,
as E M Forster said, after one has read
War and Peace for a bit, begin to sound.
There it's Russia, here it's evolution.
Everything fits intricately together,
since every species propagates as much
as it gets room for, unless limited
by predators, competitors, or climate.
Extinction is integral to the process:
transitional forms die out and leave no trace.
My hands on the steering wheel, and the eyes
with which I see road-users all around me,
have gradually arrived at what they are
through functions of which I have no remembrance.
I am a remnant with abilities
surpassing any obvious use for them,
like a bird with webbed feet far from water.
Disc Three ends and I switch from *media*
to *tuner* on the car's sound system. No point,
now, in going back to the beginning.
I park and take the shopping from the boot
and go indoors and microwave some soup.

Darwin's Man

'He must be a dull man', Darwin remarks,
'who can examine the exquisite structure
of a comb without enthusiastic
admiration.' He means the honeycomb
bees build in darkness from secreted wax.
The passage bears the hallmarks of his vision,
but we can hear something Darwin cannot –
how, a century and a half later,
those opening six words will sound to us.
First, the use of 'man' instead of 'person',
but that's the blinkers or the spectacles
of his time and culture, unremarkable
in that there are similar instances
as countless as the grains on any shore.
Second, the rare irruption into a prose
infinitely patient and objective
of emotion, the sheer rush of spirit
to the window of his intelligence,
like a child running to press *her* nose, let's say,
to chilly glass to see the first snow fall.
Third, the confidence in our common nature
that this childish wonder is what's normal,
so that to rise to high astonishment
at something most of us have never seen
or never thought about – how bees make cells,
and how perfectly they fit together,
('ingeniously', you'd say, if a craftsman
had made or a mathematician planned them)
can be predicted of us all, except
for some defective specimen, some *dull* man.

Being There

Reciting to myself again those lines
of Rilke's, relishing the guttural
ach! and prolonging it *ad lib*, I think,
if sometimes I've been tongue-tied in the presence
of a higher, more composed intelligence
than my own, how much the more completely
would I be vaporised if an angel
were suddenly to take me to its heart.
I stop short at the end of the sentence, *ich*
verginge von seinem stärkeren Dasein,
I would perish from its stronger existence.
As my OTT rendering of it
echoes between the bedroom and the bathroom,
the last word resonates in my consciousness
like an *Om,* and suddenly I notice
as if for the first time, though I cannot
really have never had this thought before,
that in German the word for existence
is not just *Sein* but *Dasein*, being *there,*
with all the freight from the Upanishads
Da has, suddenly now reconnected
with the 'give, sympathise, control' of 'What
The Thunder Said' in Eliot's *Waste Land,*
an everyday Teutonic word disclosing
its identity as holy syllable,
and Being shown to be inseparable
from a place in which to be. Space and time
they tell us, came into existence
simultaneously with the universe
at the Big Bang, and they also tell us
not to mind not understanding this, neither
do they, but I do suddenly understand,
saying *Da-sein*, hearing it echo again,
how it would be like a flash of lightning
before I was annihilated to have
an angel with its overwhelming Being

there, or here, where I pause on the landing,
having been reading and writing all morning,
badly in need of a shower and shave. *Ach*
comes later, I always forget that. I love
its vehemence so much I say it early,
and can't regret it, it seems right, there
between the supposition, if an angel,
and the consequence. *Ach!* I would be toast.

Opus 131

For Nicholas Jones, and for the Esposito Quartet

That opening slow rising-and-falling tune
on the first violin, emerging out of silence,
descending to the understanding welcome
offered by second violin, viola,
and cello so discreet I scarcely hear it,
does for me what I think the face of Jesus
must do for a suffering believer,
acknowledge all the sorrow in the world,
and with no pretence of having cancelled
the hurt and loss, and aching deprivation,
accompany courageous recognition
with a tenderness of such commensurate
proportions it seems, if not divine, human
imagination and feeling making real
for us what divinity is, or – even
for the unbeliever lurking in me,
and absolute in many other listeners –
would be, if there were such an entity.
And now, thanks to deaf Beethoven, there is.
By itself the opening minute or so
goes far beyond most other consolations,
but it gives way to a long meditation,
built on its foundation, which continues
with courage, sometimes with a forcing will,
insisting on a jerky, dancing tempo,
to say that even among tragedies
to be alive is to know gaiety,
as much as to have breath and circulation,
at other times achieving, always under
the shadow of that comprehensive vision,
which overarches the entire quartet,
sublime rhythms of serenity.
Combative struggle is not missing either.
The players urge their instruments like horses,
galloping into some desperate battle,
a rising vehemence of affirmation,

in spite of, in the teeth of, everything
that might offer to defeat and thwart us.
We are not immortal in the body,
and our lives may be cut short, broken off
by malevolence or random accident.
A day may come when hands that can execute,
ears that can hear this music will be lacking.
While we still have them, those of us gathered
in this small church in the west of Ireland,
on a gloomy day in mid–September,
feel something not unlike a candle, lit
in our collective consciousness, by us all,
signifying an immortality,
though of whom, or what, we can't be certain.

5: Visiting Giverny

Visiting Giverny

For Cathy Freeman and Jean-Paul Marot

1: Chez Monet

The House

As we move slowly, among other people,
from the entrance where we've shown our tickets
through the shop, where we will linger later,
we come back out into the early sunshine
with an intermittent view on one side
of a fantastic shout of dazzling flowers,
and on the other of the pink façade,
the background to so many garden paintings,
crowning the vista up the central path,
with the predecessors of these blooms
all around it in exuberant glory.

The studio has a doorframe for a cart
to enter, walled up now, and two large windows,
with no direct sun until the evening,
but light enough at any time of day,
certainly on this brilliant April morning.
Arrested by the pictures on the walls –
painted copies of famous originals,
and masses of Japanese prints – it's hard
to get a true sense of the space itself
as it might have been without us tourists,
queuing to move through to Monet's bedroom.
When I think to go back, to look again,
I have to wait beside the stream of people,
coming through the passage in between
one room and another, long enough
to wonder if I ought not to have bothered.

Of course we've seen pictures of it all –
the studio, the yellow dining room,

the cool kitchen with blue tiles and a row
of glowing copper pans, an instrument
you could ding from largest up to smallest,
like a wall-mounted, giant xylophone.

Jostled by other visitors, memories
of images of this house in photographs,
and of views through the windows, photographed,
and painted, too, though from another angle,
I let myself be distracted further –
suggestible as ever – like the others,
by taking a few photographs myself.

The difference it makes, coming to the house,
is how you get a sense of its proportions.
Despite the legendary rose façade,
it's not that big, or grand, or overblown.
None of the rooms could be called gigantic.
Another thing I hadn't realised –
I suppose in this it's still as it was –
is quite how many Japanese prints there are,
filling the walls the way hundreds of tulips
fill the beds outside, each specimen
undoubtedly at one time or another
singled out for attention by the eye
Cézanne said once our man was nothing but.

The Garden

The prints, massed in vertical flower beds,
solicit individual scrutiny.
Outside, the horizontal compositions,
the ranks of tulips, not so much bloom by bloom
as file by file, parade variations:
sumptuous and full, bright yellow and bright red;
white and frilly, half way to carnations;
the scarlet blooms, three to a single stem,
one budding, one full open, one half way;
white ones with petals outlined in deep pink;

and delicate, pointy-petaled specimens,
like the jester's cap on a Joker card.

There is an element of absurdity
about this whole place. It's a serious joke.
Still, though it's hard to feel it steadily
and continuously among these people,
knowing we may never come back again,
and can't experience his home as he did
in long hours of work and contemplation,
we shall take what we can from being here:
the sense of scale, big for a private garden,
though, like the house itself it's not enormous,
magnified by this density of brightness,
vibrant colours in masses large enough
to create order with their blends and contrasts
in a way that makes not a confusion
of voices, raised in fractious disputation,
but a choir like the one we heard in Wales
last week performing works by Haydn
and Mozart with trombones and cellos,
the singers' mouths opened in perfect circles,
cramming the space with harmonious thunder,
as the open goblets of these tulips
brim our consciousness with a loud Gloria.
Don't the paintings give you that themselves,
without having to see where they were made?
Yes, and no. And having long loved them, put
reproductions of them up on the walls
of several houses, today, standing here,
I say, more no than yes. Or yes, but no.

Mahler said to Bruno Walter, don't bother
Stopping to look at those, dismissing mountains,
I've already put them into music.
Mallarmé said everything existed
to end up in a book, whereas Rilke, less
provocatively, said the task of artists
like himself was to transform what was

outside into what was in the psyche,
or the imagination, or some other
word for the theatre of the spirit.
These neat beds of tulips aren't a mountain.
The natural and artificial here,
with straight paths at right angles to drilled rows,
find a more French than Austrian relation.
Monet collected bulbs as he collected
prints, and recipes, even motor cars.
Having, towards the end of a long life,
often of poverty, money to burn,
he went in for conspicuous consumption.
But if he was, round the frilly edges, made
decadent by it, his habits were fixed
and incorruptible: hard work, long hours,
during which his mind was saturated
with textures, shapes, and colours from this garden –
according to the season, irises,
chrysanthemums, roses, or these tulips.

The Other Garden

We file down steps into the underpass
and up again – the road is busy now,
and tarmacked, which was once a dusty track –
into the garden with the simple bridge,
the Japanese bridge over the famous pond.
Staff in boats are pulling up water weeds.
The guides each hold up a plastic lily
to show their status and call their groups to them.
The real lilies aren't out. There is nothing
to see but some small leaves, and not many
of them. A loud croaking sound I think's a bird
repeats, unseen. One of the gardeners
remarks to another one as they bend,
doing something to tidy up a border,
what a lot of frogs there have been lately.

The willows overhang their own reflections,
in a way that makes continuous green lines
reaching from the sky down to the depths,
and certainly recalls some of the paintings,
though I admit I see them properly
only when my daughter shows me later
the excellent photograph she took of them.
The wooden bridge is just a wooden bridge.
The pond's a pond. There are people posing.
What can I bring away? Again, the sense
of the proportions of the space, not huge,
and its relation to the tulip garden.

One of his gardeners had the job, first thing
each morning, of washing dust off the leaves
and blooms of the extravagant water lilies,
dust which blew from the road over the pond.
These days the pollution is invisible.
I overhear one of the guides explain
that every day a trailer full of plants
arrives from a nursery in the village,
to replace any that are going over.
As the guide says, there has to be always
a good show. As she doesn't need to add,
the touring parties, who have come so far
to this part of Normandy especially
to see these gardens, would be disappointed
not to feel sure they'd seen them at their best.
As we feel, regretfully departing,
but noticing the heat getting intenser
in this freak weather, after a cold spring,
glad to be leaving now and not arriving,
even though the roses aren't yet open,
any more than the iconic lilies.

Sharing a Drink

We take lunch early. We're not really hungry,
but we beat the crowds this way, and Cathy

has found a recommended place to head for.
We sit outside, four at a round table,
between the awning of the restaurant
and a miniature version of the garden
still filling our consciousness, with tulips,
fine specimens, mainly red, some yellow,
interspersed with blue forget-me-nots,
in welcome shade under a parasol.
We wouldn't usually drink till evening,
but cider here in Normandy seems perfect.
It is brought to us in an ice bucket,
expertly opened, and when we pour it
I spend some time just breathing in the perfume.

This is when I most appreciate
the aromas and associations
in my life of authentic cider, tasted
in Somerset and then in Normandy,
my first encounters with intoxicants,
in the presence of my parents, both of them
in England, and with Dad cycling in France.
How delicious that lunchtime glass had been,
and how surprised I was to find my legs
had turned to lead, heavy and unresponsive,
when we started again and faced a climb.

Now I know the potency of liquor,
but that's not why I am abstaining, just
that I'm tasting the bouquet so fully.
I remember Yeats's lines about the ghosts
able to savour the fume of Muscatel,
and I imagine myself in company
with the poet and his unseen friends, himself
a spirit now, and myself, as I wrote once
years ago, in this like any adult,
already partly my own ghost. Only
later does it occur to me what or who
makes me linger so long, aligning myself
with august spirits of the departed.

Who's breathing in the scent of apples with me,
giving his sharpened palate ecstasy?
Someone who has been present all this morning,
someone who presided at the table
in the yellow dining room and remembered,
looking outside, that in his first years here
where the tulips are was apple orchard.

2: Monet and Friends

In the Giverny gallery the painting
by Monet, of two houses in the snow
under a snow-laden sky, dominates
pictures by his contemporaries because
he has made light shine, the texture vibrant,
in every centimetre of the canvas.

In a second room his imitators
present scenes that he had also treated,
but the picture you can't take your eyes off
does not depict the pond, gardens, or house,
but sunset over the Channel at Pourville.
The life jumps out at you from all of it.
Monet was only an eye? It is the mind
that shines through the effects of changing light.

3: In Vernon

These photographs from the eighteen-nineties
were taken here, in this *département*
of Normandy where it borders Paris,
which contains Giverny and, nearby, Vernon.
It is called l'Eure, a name I have to ask
the *gardien* to repeat and to spell out.
When he does I thank him, adding politely,
il faut être à l'heure, I just can't help it.
One must be on time; even, up to date.

And we should absolutely be in this place.
Things that strike me about these photographs
by Paul Fagas: how very dark and heavy
men and women's clothes were always, even
on what must have been warm days; and how pinched,
ancient, and joyless children's faces look,
toughened and wizened. How practical and dark,
and heavy, and without a hint of charm,
their own clothes are, and how completely black,
dense and voluminous the smoke is, rising
from steam engines passing across landscapes.
The group of charcoal burners, standing near
a black heap of their product on bare ground,
look unglamorous and unromantic.
But the rivers, with their reeds and waterfowl,
are still the same today as they were then,
at least to look at in a photograph.

The dates move forward, nineteen hundred, nineteen
hundred and three, the year my dad was born
in the East End, while the young Edward Thomas
mirrored the English countryside in prose,
though often overworked, depressed, and poor.
How heavy the constraints were there, and here,
where Monet, heavy himself by this time,
present in this exhibition in its title
but not in any of the images,
wore, in all the photographs I can think of,
thick, formal clothes at odds with all the lightness,
the weightlessness his paintings work to conjure.

These would seem, in retrospect, the good times,
at least to some, and by comparison.
The day before coming to Giverny
we walked in woods beside the river Marne,
grateful for the shade of towering trees,
watching fish, cormorants, and water-hens,
like these photographed on the Seine by Fagas,
and saw the pillars of a vanished bridge,

bringing to mind the battles fought there, one
in nineteen fourteen, one four years later,
years of unimaginable slaughter.

4: After Monet

Why should it make a difference, seeing again
this reproduction of a Monet painting
of his Japanese garden with its bridge
over a pond under weeping willows,
a composition in greens, blues, and yellows
which has been on our wall for several months,
now that we've walked over that little bridge
and round that garden? I don't know whether
the shock new knowledge brings will be a prelude
to anything that could be called an insight,
or just something superficial – *been there* –
an illusion of ownership or closeness,
like that of some of the other visitors
crowding the bridge, having their photos taken.

In this painting that bridge seems to float, not
on the water but in the air. The ends,
which raise it from the earth and bring it down,
are cut off by the picture frame, as they might be
in a print from Japan on Monet's wall.
It's yellower on the right than on the left,
suggesting sunlight on a summer morning,
as do the leaves and blossoms of the lilies,
and the weepers of the burdened willows
which crowd the picture space, and yet recede,
as if the pond with its surrounding trees
might be a river, not just fed by one,
stretching indefinitely through a forest.

We were too early for the waterlilies,
but we can't forget now how prosaic
and simple that bridge was, made of timber,

painted green, perfectly ordinary.
The willows were lovely; willows tend to be.
That garden wasn't tiny, but it's smaller
than you would imagine from the picture,
tamer perhaps, less overbrimmed with life –
but we were there in April, not July.

What do I see I didn't see before?
The solid underpinning of what's there,
its three dimensions, its substantial Being.
The sense of weightlessness, and of extent
obscured and yet implied by the four edges
of the canvas, is now counterpointed
by a greater sense of incarnation
as well as spatial limits. The energy
materiality and presence possess
made it worth the bother of going there.

The artist's transformation of the scene
is the more remarkable, seeing how much
of the value that makes us wish to look,
and go on looking with deep satisfaction,
is added to the *motif* that he worked with.
The ideal viewer would extrapolate
this understanding from experience
of what it is to walk round any garden.
But which of us is an ideal viewer?
Not me. I see better, now I've been there.

5: Something That Has Flowered

Surprisingly foggy first thing, after heat
yesterday, and with more promised today.
Glancing up, I see the apple blossom
now coming out below the newly open
cascading trailers of the weeping birch.
The fuzzy blobs of pink and white and red
among the dominant greens, some light, some dark –

for a moment I'm back in Giverny,
where the water lilies weren't in bloom yet,
although the weeping willows were in leaf,
when we were there two weeks ago, and in
the National Gallery, Trafalgar Square,
where I was the day before yesterday,
and where the water lilies were resplendent.
The canvas I stood sometimes right up close to,
and sometimes further back from, had the texture
of this scene, indistinctly luminous,
as reassuringly rugged and rough
as the bark of an ancient apple tree,
and these living colours, exactly these.
It is more than just being reminded.
Still not fully awake, for a minute
I don't know where I am, I'm free of knowing,
still processing the bright information
which will tell me. Why should this be precious,
this interval of not yet understanding,
waking up to something that has flowered?
My dreams have been vivid and plausible,
and I have had to keep on readjusting.
Good preparation for looking outside
and thinking I am seeing nenuphars.
The light is changing, as it used to change,
of course, in the gardens at Giverny.

6: Time Perpetually Revolving

Double Take

For Mike James

I'd forgotten how extremely tall he is,
how big, how very solidly built, and strong.
He stands in front of me and I look up
as a Victorian little boy might lift his gaze
from the gold chain across a breathing waistcoat.
I tilt my head back, see the mountaintop
with the sun rising at the back of it.
No, it's a face, radiating comfort,
a blazing log fire in a coaching inn
on a wet afternoon or frosty night.
'You don't know who I am, do you?' A voice
comes down from the mountain. 'Not yet', I say,
but I will in a minute.' Then he tells me
we used to walk round Thompson's Park, talking,
when he and Angela lived one side of it
and I lived on the other. It's a fine park,
but strolling round it by whatever route
doesn't take long, and sometimes we'd go twice
rather than stop talking to each other.
Mike understood so much about the world
I hadn't tumbled to, and no doubt still does.
He's still active, spends even more of his time
out of doors now he's retired from teaching.
Maybe that's why he seems even sunnier.
His company is like a joy transfusion,
a roaring fire. A mountaintop. The sun.

Putting the Clock Back

For Antonia Gransden

We hadn't tried to warn her we were coming. It seemed simpler just to arrive, having told her daughter at least, who would have warned us if there was some reason not to visit on that particular morning at that time.

The door of her room was open, so we walked in, and said who we were in case she didn't – she probably didn't, in fact – recognise us. She answered us in the end quite clearly but very quietly, so we strained to listen, reading her face and letting her read our own expressions. I took care to keep mine mobile, not drop into rigidity, glazed over, while waiting for the pebbles we dropped into the deep well of her consciousness to return the delayed echo of her thoughtful answers. You learn to slow down in such circumstances. We sent our messages to her distant planet and waited for them to arrive and be decoded, and for the precious signs of lively thinking, like evidence of life on Mars, to be collected and transmitted, and to travel and reach us through the miles of frozen darkness.

The line was good. Her voice didn't break up, except on two or three occasions when her face did and she cried like a small child, silently, knowing it is loved but feeling the pain as of fingers, say, caught between a door and the frame it is closing into. I cry, she said, when I get emotional. Some at least of her tears were happy, as when she took in our surprise arrival. Her crying made us all more intimate, putting us in touch with our own inner infant, with our memories of being ill and tearful, and of seeing other people we have loved, emotional in illness or old age, or at some crisis. My mum and dad were surrogate mum and dad to her when she was a disconsolate teen before I was born, her parents having parted. She gave me sheepskin slippers once when she spent Christmas with us. Cor, I said, it's like walking on clouds. When my mother said again, quite frankly, and paused, our visitor laughed, and said, I know if someone starts a sentence that way they're going to say something horrible. She knew my mum all right, as well as I did. Another time – she had two children, and was married three times – in conversation someone must have evoked a youthful image of her as a girl, a maiden, virginal: *that* would be putting the clock back, she said, drily. Listening to her, talking to her, smiling, I let the clock run backwards in my head.

Comfort for My Aunt

For Wynne Martin

Can you make me better, my aunt says,
smiling at the doctor who is standing
at the foot of her bed, knowing the answer,
and manifesting no agitation,
almost teasing him because he cannot,
and we all know it, that's why my brother
and I have come all this way to see her.
It's a mark of her character, her style,
to say with such composure, such good grace
and so many layers of implication,
lightly, can you make me better, with a smile,
hinting gaily, though she's ninety something,
at a girlish mockery, and the doctor,
without showing if he does or doesn't
appreciate the richness of the moment,
gives without a beat his practised come-back,
I can make you more comfortable, and then
I hear more clearly retrospectively
in my aunt's question something in her wishing,
as we all might, to believe in miracles,
or never having lost the certainty
that there is nothing to be done to save her,
wanting at least tacitly acknowledged
what nobody will say, that it's a pity.

Time Perpetually Revolving

for Anne Cluysenaar

I pick up a book of verse whose author
I had known for thirty years and more
when she died suddenly six months ago.
The poem it opens on moves back in time
a few years to a herd of cows dispersed,
no longer swinging past the local windows
at milking time, an hour or two from dusk,
then, by way of 'pock-marked, shell-packed' siltstone
in a copse 'muffling the tock of hammers' –
geologists on a field trip, I gather –
visualises the reality
of how what is now that landscape must have been
when it was under sea, a period
so long ago the noughts are meaningless
to imagination: the Silurian.
In Anne's poem she never leaves her reader
without something to see or touch or hear,
and comes back to the present and the future,
and the image of herself, for a whole
long, hot afternoon in August watching,
as she tells us, through binoculars, a hatching
of Clouded Yellows, 'the vehement zigzag
of wings'. 'And yet', she adds, 'by winter, all
will be dead'. As she was, by last winter.
Rereading these lines brings her back to me,
alive, in a composite portrait of her
as she was across the years I knew her.
I see an image which has been gestating
for several weeks through other meditations,
ready to hatch at last, of time like cards
in the hands of an ambidextrous dealer,
being cascaded evenly from one
hand to the other, and then back again,
each moment a card, my contemplation
moving lightly backward and forward through them,
evenly spaced, the corner of each showing

as it follows, followed in succession,
all of the past and all the future living
all the time, perpetually revolving,
with Anne steadily present to my mind,
like a face given back by moving water.

Winging It

For Gwyn Ingli James

Flat on his back and tangled in a sheet,
his jaw sagging, his eyes slightly open,
the architecture showing through his face,
he might have been already a cadaver.
Slowly he roused, and while she went on speaking
began to whisper words hard to decipher.
She asked my help to shift him slightly upwards.
He's got no strength in his muscles, she said,
and his bones ache. He was restless, scrabbling
towards one sock and then towards the other.
One was rucked under his heel and instep,
which must have been uncomfortable. I pulled
both of them up, talking as I did so,
but later he slipped one of them off.

By that time we were conversing, more or less.
He mentioned the word joke, somebody once,
he seemed to be remembering, had told
him one, so I said, well, a joke's a joke,
and that hit the spot and got him going
with new urgency, and though I only heard
part of what he said, and made sense of less,
somehow the two of us kept the ball rolling.
Violence, he said clearly at one point.
The world's in a terrible state, I said,
but then it always was, and he agreed,
and seemed to wish he had done more about it,
and I said what he'd given his life to doing,
inspiring generations of young people,
was doing something wonderful about it.
The consequences would go on for ever.
Then I reminded him of fellow teachers
we used to know, the ones he was friends with,
the ones who made our lives a misery.
How lucky we were now not to have to
put up with them, the way we used to daily.

I quoted things he sometimes said to me,
the poems he recited to his students.
His voice strengthened, he smiled, answered questions.

From where I was standing now his face
looked handsome – it had always had good structure –
and his hair lay as if it had been styled.
I said he made me think of Omar Sharif.
I expect you're getting tired, I said at last,
you need to rest. He said clearly, yes. By now
I was holding both his hands in both of mine.

Afterwards I wondered what had happened.
The thing I haven't said is that I laughed.
I put myself aside, let not just the love,
but the effervescence bubble through me,
the indestructible, motherly joy.
I noticed I was still in overdrive
when friendly neighbours later greeted me
in the supermarket and I answered,
leaving them slightly breathless, overwhelmed
by my larger-than-life enthusiasm.
I found the energy for a short walk
though it was close and I knew I was fading,
and got home crumpled, grumpy and exhausted,
kept humble by encountering my limits,
having played host to something rather spacious
in which I had no rights of ownership.

Crossing the Ravine

For Joan James

He looked so peaceful, she says again, and I
remind her, not that she needs reminding,
she wrote down one of his coherent phrases,
I need something to give me peace. Both times
I saw him he was restless and seemed troubled,
but in the last few days he was more tranquil.
The Marie Curie nurses were marvellous,
she says, as she has also said before,
while we followed not the progress but the course
of what there has been for a long time no
mistaking was the last stage of his illness.
It's always a shock when it happens, I say,
no matter how much it has been expected.
I said goodbye to him each night, she tells me,
in case it was the last time I would see him.

Their daughter came to stay for the weekend,
but when she said she would be going soon
he made such a face she knew she wouldn't,
and found she could increasingly sit with him,
deeply content in this companionship
even though he was largely unconscious.
As she was there her mother could go out
to do a little necessary shopping
on Thursday in the middle of the morning.
I don't mind, she says, I don't mind, meaning
that she wasn't there for those last moments.
I think her absence may have granted him
the necessary space and loneliness
to slip away, not that she hadn't given
her permission to him to depart in peace.

Still, she is grieving, and he knew she would.
Their daughter too, but as she lives elsewhere
that was perhaps more like a parting gift,
from her to him, accepted, him to her.

He died at home, she says, among his books.
It's what he wanted, and I know she's right.
I know too that all these consolations,
his looking peaceful, not being in pain,
dying at home, are her attempts, partly
successful, but never completely so,
to make her own peace, make something creative,
like one of her exquisite, subtle haiku,
out of her yearning emptiness and grief.
They're like, I think, an oriental painting,
her consoling thoughts – how marvellous
the nurses were, and all the love around her,
and how he lay at home so peacefully –
of a picturesque but flimsy bridge,
a woman, maybe wearing a kimono,
or a tonsured, pigtailed pilgrim with a staff,
is crossing, over a ravine so deep
all you can see below is rocks and mist.

Celebrating the Life

For Jean-Jacques Gabas

1: The Artist

Nothing to celebrate, he said one birthday.
Only half laughing, he added that he wanted
a statue on his grave, himself reclining,
thumbing his nose at the divinity.
Life gives everybody a wound, perhaps,
to spend their years partly overcoming,
those of us, at least, with enough good luck
not to be crushed completely early on.
His overcoming was spectacular.
As I told him yesterday, no-one I know
has personified the art of living
better than he has done, and few come close.
His joy in scholarship, and art, and music,
teaching, travel, food and wine, and friendship,
has prompted many to surpass themselves.
Today he writes that till recently he spent
a long time on the internet exploring,
with great pleasure, some of the photographs
of Florentine and Roman churches. Now,
he adds, he tends to doze off. 'But memories
hover above, and they're warming and glowing,
without a hint of bitterness or regret.'
As I wrote in my reply, difficult
to start, and more difficult to finish,
he's rising to the last and hardest challenge
for a past master in the art of living,
showing us by example what it is
to master too the tricky art of dying,
leaving in our perishable hearts
a better legacy than an edition,
or a recumbent statue on a tombstone.

2: Last Call

I can write another time about the content
of Jean-Jacques' email, which was so moving –
the evidence will still be in my inbox.
But what I must record, though time is pressing,
before it fades is the auditory trace
of hearing his voice on the phone, so himself,
so rich and velvety and civilized,
and slightly accented for all the years,
half a century, he's lived in Wales.
It's the first time I've heard that voice for months,
since last we went to lunch with him and Ieuan,
and possibly the last time ever, though,
listening, you would not guess how far, now,
the illness has advanced, and he assures me
he feels quite peaceful, and the agitation
in which he wrote to me has passed. He's had
a long and happy life, and when I say
he's an inspiration to us all, he says
an old fool is still a fool to the end,
and I can't help laughing, and I tell him
that it's just like him to make me more
cheerful rather than less, and leave me giggling.
We send each other love, and I promise
to phone again when I come back, although
we both know he may by then be beyond
taking my call, or knowing if I made one.

3: Cézanne at the National Portrait Gallery

We three share our insights, and we have some,
but all the time a silent friend is with me,
someone who spent not hours but many days
taking notes in other exhibitions.
He travelled Europe just to see Cézannes.
I was confident he would be famous.
Who was it said he put his talent into

his art, his genius into living?
Of course, it must have been Oscar, and Jean-Jacques
had something of Wilde's wit and his flamboyance,
his all-round culture and sophistication,
with a warmth and gentleness that was his own.
He could have answered anything we asked,
questions rising in us as we focused
on painting after painting, and the wording
on the helpful notices beside them.
I've felt his absence sorely all this morning.
'He might have been your heartiest welcomer'
and our most entertaining, wise explainer.
It was the proper place to be, of all days
on this, when just before leaving the hotel
to come here, in a rush, running late, I found
an email telling me that, with a nurse present,
he died last night, and that he did not suffer.

4: A Moment Sketched

He was telling me about the funeral,
how the old ladies came to shake his hand,
and here he did a stylized imitation
of their nodding heads, bowed down with the years
and with a grief they almost seemed to relish,
to judge from his rendition, barking
as if through sobs, it will come to us all,
ça nous arrivera tous. It was so vivid,
his little sketch, that all these years later,
trying to find him in my memories,
this one brings me closer than most others,
and in its wake I hear him moving on
in his own more usual way of talking
to say that though in fact it was he
who was more grief-stricken than anyone,
he found himself having to comfort them,
these dowagers, making a meal of it,
self-centredness they took for something else

173

skewered in retrospect by his performance,
but at the time, when he had needed kindness,
adding to his cares and his distresses.
Of course they were thinking of their own
proximity to death, and he and I
knew, theoretically, that we were mortal,
but it was too far down the things to do,
item umpteen on our own agendas,
the last before the letters AOB,
for us to hear as more than notional.
Ça nous arrivera tous. My dear Jean-Jacques,
I hear and see your little bit of acting
so vividly that, though I know it has,
I can't believe it has happened to you.
Any other business? Date of next meeting?
Perhaps you're reunited with the mother
whose death you never quite recovered from.

5: My Daughter Answers a Question

'I certainly do remember him! I remember
someone very intelligent and learned,
vastly *érudit,** and very stylish
in a positive way, as in, brought up
with good manners he had cultivated,
the way he used to cultivate his melons –
or tomatoes, or whatever it was –
in Cucuron, *un intellectuel
bourgeois,* enlightened by the simplicity
only the real ones can afford (as opposed
to '*la culture c'est comme la confiture,
moins tu en as, plus tu l'étales*'). I recall
going to his elegant place near Cardiff
with you and others, his big dog (or dogs?),
and the delicious food, the lovely wine.
It was he, I'm certain, who informed me
I had the syndrome of the '*haricot vert
qui se prend pour une aubergine.*' I do

remember him, someone I would have liked
to spend more time with, somebody from whom
you always felt you could learn more, a very
generous and genuine *professeur.*
To sum up, I remember him with details
some of which may be a bit approximate,
but with a fondness which there's no mistaking.'

And, Cathy, you have prompted me to see you,
and your sister, when you were young children,
and we went with your mother to Cucuron,
having grown restless as the adults chatted,
magically calmed when Jean-Jacques led you both,
each of you slipping a hand into his,
to see and sample melons or tomatoes.
I see the three of you as in a painting,
returning into view, his spell still holding,
having revealed another of his talents,
one I might otherwise not have suspected.

I wonder whether anyone could count them,
the different ways in which his one light shone.

*The French words in italics in this section can be roughly translated, in the order of
their appearance above: learned; a middle-class intellectual; culture is like jam, the
less you have, the more you spread it; a runner bean mistaking itself for an
aubergine; teacher.*

Two Women

For Martyn Caira, and IM Ruth Calway

Six of us sat round a little table.
The young women were strangers to each other.
One of them had brought her parents with her.
Everybody was on best behaviour.

It was summer. There was a crawling wasp.
One woman turned a tumbler upside down
over the wasp to stop it interfering
with the sugar on our little cakes.

When attention had drifted back again
to the conversation we were sharing
the other woman playfully inserted
a makeshift wedge under the glass's rim.

It wasn't so big that the wasp could crawl out,
but big enough for fresh air to get in.
She didn't want it to asphyxiate.
We exchanged a fleeting and unnoticed smile.

That was years ago. The woman with the parents
got in touch again just before Christmas.
She sent warm greetings and her latest news.
She seems to be well launched in her career.

Something I read reminded me this morning
of that other woman. It's a letter
Rilke wrote about Vera Knoop, the dancer.
This harmonious being-one of her heart, he writes,

opened to everything… this joyful, this
much-moved, this to ultimate capacity
belonging way into the here and now…
No… into the whole, into a far more than here

and now...how she reached with her heart's antennae
out beyond everything here graspable...
I had begun to think of our friend already,
and of her care for every living creature.

Then that word *antennae* brought the moment
of her solicitude for the trapped wasp
back to me as if we were all present.
As the sentence I was reading went on

it called up another scene, last summer,
in our own garden, when she visited.
We all knew she would not live much longer,
but not that this was the last time we'd see her.

In her light melodious voice, and smiling,
she said she hoped her sense of breathlessness
was just a chest infection. It wasn't.
But that day she filled us with joyousness.

Oh yes, the sentence I was quoting from.
It goes on: *in those sweet hovering pauses*
in pain that, full of the dream of recovery,
were still granted her... That's it. That was her.

How Are You Going to Live?

For Rhiannon Jones

They will all die one day and so will you.
You may think that what is past is gone
as if it had never been. You may believe
death is the final end of everything
for the person dying. Suppose you are right:
how are you going to live out your life? I
choose to live mine as if everything good
that happens will shine everlastingly. As if
heaven were the act of giving-receiving,
where it's impossible to say which of us
gives and which receives, but in this act,
in the energy passing between us,
we become, without losing our own
identities, one with each other, one
with giving. Our act – you can see how
the myth-makers felt – becomes a new
constellation in the night sky, there
whenever anyone chooses to look up.